Low-Carb Slow Cooker Classics

Low-Carb Slow Cooker Classics

Healthy Dinners That Are Ready When You Are!

Dana Carpender

APPLE

Text © 2005 by Dana Carpender

First published in the UK in 2005 by
Apple Press
7 Greenland Street
London NW1 0ND
United Kingdom

www.apple-press.com

Reprinted in 2007, 2008, 2009

08 07 06 05 04 1 2 3 4 5

ISBN 978-1-84092-483-1

Library of Congress Cataloging-in-Publication Data available

Cover design by Mary Ann Smith
Book design by Leslie Haimes

Printed and bound in Finland

For my sister Kim,

who works way too hard,

and loves her slow cooker.

C O N T E N T S

Introduction:
My Journey to Slow Cooker Mastery

I have a confession: When my editor, Holly, suggested I write a low-carb slow cooker book, I baulked. Oh, I knew it would be popular – many readers had written to me asking for a slow cooker book. I just wasn't thrilled at the idea of a couple of months of slow-cooked dinners. I'd made some slow-cooked meals that were pretty good, but overall, it seemed to me that most slow-cooked food was not brilliant. Too many dishes seemed to be waterlogged, mushy, and insipid. Furthermore, so many slow cooker recipes seemed to rely on high-carb tinned cream soups – indeed, many slow cooker books seemed to think that 'put food in pot, throw in condensed cream-of-mushroom soup, and cook on low until you come home from work' was a recipe – but not in my book, figuratively or literally!

So I resisted for quite a while, but those e-mails saying, 'Please, please, write us a slow cooker book!' were piling up in my inbox. I needed to write a slow cooker book! But it was clear I had to get better at slow cooking.

Well, my mum is a retired librarian, and from her I learnt years ago that if you want to learn something, you need to look it up. So I went to Amazon.com and read reviews of slow cooker books to determine which were drawing raves. I then read the books that got the best reviews, gleaning what I could from them of the tricks of making slow cooker food as appealing as possible, both in taste and texture. Not surprisingly, my slow-cooker performance took a remarkable upturn!

I also got an idea of what slow cookers do well. Obviously, they're not for anything that you want to come out crispy and brown, but if what you need is slow, moist cooking, a slow cooker will do it better than any other appliance. Preparing soups and stews and braising are obvious slow cooker strengths, but I also learned that a slow cooker is terrific for cooking anything that needs to be baked in a water bath (sometimes called a bain-marie) – custards, in particular. I was thrilled to discover that my slow cooker did the best job ever of roasting nuts and seeds, and it's perfect for hot beverages for parties and hors d'oeuvres that would otherwise need a chafing dish.

I was very surprised to learn that cooking fish in my slow cooker worked well. You can't leave it for hours and hours because fish overcooks easily. But just an hour or so of the gentle heat of the slow cooker leaves fish tender, moist, and succulent. Do try it when you have an hour to get dinner on the table, even if you mostly use your slow cooker to cook supper while you're out of the house for hours.

I also had a few spectacular failures. (Don't even ask about the brussels sprouts!) But overall, I was pleased to discover that with a few simple considerations in mind, slow cookers can turn out truly wonderful food.

About Slow Cookers

By the time I finished this project, I owned three slow cookers. All of them are Rival Crock-Pots, the original slow cooker. (Crock-Pot is a brand name. All Crock-Pots are slow cookers, but not all slow cookers are Crock-Pots.) The best slow cookers are ones where the heat comes from all around the crockery insert, rather than only coming from the bottom. If you have one of the slow cookers that has the heating element only on the bottom, you'll have to experiment a bit with these recipes to see if the times are correct.

The 'low' setting on a Rival Crock-Pot is around 200°F (just above, actually, because things will boil eventually at this setting, and the boiling point is 212°F), and the 'high' setting is around 300°F. If you have another brand of slow cooker that lets you set specific temperatures, keep this in mind. If you have another brand of slow cooker and you're not sure what temperature the settings will give (look in the booklet that came with it for this information), you can fill the slow cooker with water, heat it for 2 hours on low, and test the water's temperature with a kitchen thermometer, but this is a lot of trouble. I'd probably just use the low and high settings and keep mental notes on how meals turn out.

The best slow cookers have crockery inserts that lift out of the base. This allows them to be refrigerated, microwaved (if your microwave is big enough), and – most important – put in the dishwasher. *Do not* put your slow cooker in the dishwasher if the crockery cannot be separated from the heating element! Nothing electric should ever be submerged in water.

My slow cookers range in size. The smallest holds 2.5 litres, the middle-sized holds 3 litres, while the big one holds 5 litres. The 5 litre tin easily holds enough food for 8 people. It's the obvious choice if you have a big family or like to cook enough to have left-overs for future meals. The 3 litre is the most common size. If you have a family of 4, it should be about right. If you have this size, you'll need to halve recipes that make 6 to 8 servings. The 2 1/2 litre is great for making dips, hot hors d'oeuvres, and hot beverages, but it is a bit small for family cooking.

Another consideration: My 5 litre slow cooker will fit a 1 1/2 litre casserole dish or 20cm springform pan, opening up many new cooking options. If you have a smaller unit and want to make custards, cheesecakes, and other dishes that call for inserting a dish or pan, you'll have to find dishes that will fit. It's easier with a bigger slow cooker.

Keep in mind that slow cookers come in round or oval shapes. You'll want a round slow cooker, instead of an oval, so you can insert a round glass casserole or a springform. Sadly, a big, round slow cooker takes the most storage space. I know of no good way around this.

Some Things I've Learned about Slow Cooking

- Browning meat or poultry before putting it in the slow cooker upgrades vast hordes of recipes. Yes, it takes time and dirties up a skillet. But the flavour and texture that browning bring are worth it, worth it, worth it. Often I'll have you sauté your vegetables, too.

- It's important to keep liquids to the minimum that will make the recipe work, especially in recipes that have a lot of vegetables. All of the liquid that cooks out of the food while slow cooking will accumulate in the pot because no evaporation occurs. It's easy to end up with very watery food. This rule does not apply to soups, of course.

- Because of this accumulation of liquid, it's a good idea to use concentrated flavours. In particular, you'll find that in many of these recipes I use both stock and bouillon concentrate to make what amounts to a stock that is double-strength or more.

- Sometimes it's a good idea to transfer the liquid from the slow cooker to a saucepan and boil it hard till it's reduced by half. Half the volume means double the flavour.

- It's generally best to use lean cuts of meat, and you'll see I've often used skinless poultry, too. This is because fat that becomes crackling and succulent in the oven makes slow-cooker food unbearably greasy. This makes slow cooking a great way to cook some of the leaner and tougher cuts of meat that you might not want to roast. It also makes slow cooking a good cooking method for those of you who are watching calories as well as carbs. It can even save you money – often tough and bony cuts of meat are cheap.

- For some strange reason, vegetables cook more slowly in a slow cooker than meat does. If you put vegetables on top of the meat in your slow cooker, you may find that they're still crunchy when the rest of the dinner is done. Put the ingredients in the pot in the order given in the recipes in this book.

- For this reason, too, it's best to cut vegetables into fairly small pieces. You'll find I've told you what size to cut things, for the most part. If the recipe says 2cm cubes, and you cut your turnips in 5cm cubes, you're going to have underdone turnips.

- It's never a bad idea to spray your slow cooker with oil to prevent sticking before putting the food in it. I don't always do this, though I've specified it where it seems a particularly good idea. But I can't think of a situation in which it would hurt.

Things That Other Slow Cooker Books Seem to Think Are Terribly Important, But Don't Seem Like a Big Deal to Me

- Several books wanted me to use only whole spices, such as whole peppercorns or coarse-cracked pepper, whole cloves, whole leaf herbs, etc., etc. I used what I had on hand. I got tasty food.

- A few books felt that you shouldn't season your slow cooker food until the end of cooking time. I do often suggest that you add salt and pepper to taste at the end of the cooking time, but other than that, our seasonings go into the pot with the food. I've never had a problem with this.

- Some books were emphatic about the size of the slow cooker. This matters some; you can't put 4 litres of soup in a 3-litre slow cooker, and if you're only making a small batch of dip, you probably shouldn't use a 5 1/2-litre pot. But some cookbooks predicted dire results if I didn't fill my slow cooker at least halfway. I often filled my big slow cooker less than halfway. And I got tasty food.

About Timing

The biggest reason for the popularity of slow cookers is what I call 'time-shifting' – the fact that they allow you to cook dinner at a time other than right before you eat it, so you can eat soon after you get home from work. Because of this, many slow cooker books tell you to cook most of their recipes for 8 hours or more. They figure you'll be away that long.

Unfortunately, I find that many dishes get unbearably mushy and overdone if they cook that long. I've tried to give the cooking times that I feel give the best results, which may not be the time that fits with your working day. These can generally be extended by an hour without a problem, but extending them by 2, 3, or more hours may well give you a very different result than I got.

A better idea is to do all your prep work the night before – cooking dinner after dinner, as it were. Then lift the filled crockery insert out of the base and stash it in the fridge overnight. The next morning, pull it out of the fridge, put it in the base, and turn it on, just before you leave the house. Starting with chilled food will add 1 to 2 hours to your cooking time. If you do this, don't heat up the base before putting the chilled crockery insert in! You may well crack the crockery.

If you need to extend your time even further, consider getting a timer. You should be fine letting your food wait 2 hours before the timer turns on the slow cooker – 3 if the food is straight out of the fridge when the crockery goes in the base. It's a better idea to delay the starting time than to turn the pot off early because retained heat will cause the food to continue cooking even after the pot is turned off. Ask the nice people at your local hardware shop about a timer you can plug things into. If you're just now acquiring your slow cooker, there are units available with time-delayed starters built in.

On the other hand, if you want to speed up a slow cooker recipe, you can do so by getting the contents warm before putting the crockery insert in the base. The crocks for two of my three slow cookers fit in my microwave. I have, on occasion, microwaved the crock on medium heat until it was warm through before putting the crock in the base to continue cooking. This cuts a good hour off the cooking time.

You can, of course, also use the high setting when the low setting is specified. This will cut the cooking time roughly in half. However, I find that for most recipes low yields better results. If you have the time to use it when it's recommended, I suggest you do so.

If you're going to be around for a while and leave the house later, you could cook on high for an hour or so, then switch to low when you leave. Figure, again, that each hour on high is worth 2 hours on low.

The size of your slow cooker relative to your recipe will somewhat affect the cooking time. If you have a 5 1/2-litre slow cooker and the food only fills it ¼ full, you can likely subtract 1 hour from the cooking time. Conversely, if the food fills your slow cooker to within an inch of the rim, you can add an hour.

Ingredients
Common and Not So Common Ingredients

Here, in alphabetical order, are a few ingredients I thought needed a little explanation:

- **_Beer_** – One or two recipes in this book call for beer. The lowest carbohydrate beer on the market is Michelob Ultra, but I don't much like it. Still, it should be okay for cooking. Miller Lite and Milwaukee's Best Light are better, and they have only about 0.5 grams more carb per can.

- **_Black soybeans_** – Most beans and other legumes are too high in carbohydrates for many low-carb dieters, but there is one exception. Black soybeans have a very low usable carb count, about 1 gram per serving, because most of the carbs in them are fibre.

   I wouldn't recommend eating soybean recipes several times a week. I know that soy has a reputation for being the Wonder Health Food of All Existence, but there are reasons to be cautious. For decades now, soy has been known to be hard on the thyroid, and if you're trying to lose weight and improve your health, a slow thyroid is the last thing you need. More alarmingly, a study done in Hawaii in 2000 showed a correlation between the amount of tofu subjects ate in middle age and their rate and severity of cognitive problems in old age. Because scientists suspect the problem lies with the soy estrogens that have been so highly touted, any unfermented soy product, including tinned soybeans, is suspect.

   This doesn't mean we should completely shun soybeans and soy products, but we need to approach them with caution and eat them in moderation. Because many low-carb speciality products are soy-heavy, you'll want to pay attention there, too. Personally, I try to keep my soy consumption to 1 serving a week or less.

- **_Black Treacle_** – What on earth is treacle doing in a low-carb cookbook?! It's practically all carbohydrate, after all. Well, yes, but I've found that combining Splenda with a very small amount of treacle gives a good, brown-sugar flavour to all sorts of recipes. Always use the darkest treacle you can find. The darker it is, the stronger the flavour, and the lower the carb count. That's why I specify black treacle, the darkest, strongest treacle there is. It's nice to know that black treacle is also where all the minerals they take out of sugar end up. It may be high-carb, but at least it's not a nutritional wasteland. Still, I use only small amounts.

Most health food stores carry black treacle, but if you can't get it, buy the darkest treacle you can find. Most supermarket brands come in both light and dark varieties.

Why not use some of the artificial brown-sugar flavoured sweeteners out there? Because I've tried them, and I haven't tasted one I would be willing to buy again.

- **Stocks** – Tinned or packaged chicken stock and beef stock are very handy items to keep around and certainly quicker than making your own. However, the quality of most of ready-made stock you'll find at your local supermarket is appallingly bad. The chicken stock has all sorts of chemicals in it, and often sugar as well. The beef stock is worse. It frequently has no beef in it whatsoever. I refuse to use these products, and you should, too.

  However, there are a few tinned or boxed stocks on the market worth buying. Many supermarkets now carry fresh stock, and a brand called Kallo, which contains no chemicals at all. Kallo comes in chicken and beef. Health food stores also have good quality tinned and boxed stocks. The Marigold brand is widely distributed in the UK.

  Decent packaged stock will cost you a little more than the stuff that is made of salt and chemicals, but not a much more. If you watch for sales, you can often get it as cheaply as the bad stuff, so stock up. When my health food store runs a sale on good stock, I buy piles of it!

  ONE LAST NOTE: You will also find tinned vegetable stock, particularly at health food stores. This is tasty, but because it runs much higher in carbohydrates than chicken and beef stocks, I'd avoid it.

- **Bouillon or stock concentrates** – Bouillon or stock concentrate comes in cubes, crystals, liquids, and pastes. It is generally full of salt and chemicals and doesn't taste notably like the animal it supposedly came from. Kallo stock cubes are the best of the bunch. These concentrates definitely do *not* make a suitable substitute for good quality stock if you're making a pot of soup. However, they can be useful for adding a little kick of flavour here-and there – more as seasonings than as soups. For this use, I keep them on hand.

- *Cauliflower* – You'll notice a certain reliance on cauliflower in this book, both in the form of 'Fauxtatoes' (see recipe page 239) and in the form of Cauli-Rice (see recipe page 239). This is because many slow cooker recipes make wonderful gravy, and it's a shame not to have a side dish to help you eat it. (Indeed, traditional slow cooker recipes show a similar dependence on potatoes, rice, and noodles.)

    You can skip the cauliflower if you like. Or you can substitute low-carb pasta from time to time, though I haven't found a brand I really like yet.

    BY THE WAY: If cauliflower (or another suggested garnish or side dish) isn't mentioned in the ingredient list, it's merely suggested and it's not included in the nutritional analysis for the dish. If it is in the ingredient list, it has been included in the analysis.

- *Chilli garlic paste* – This is a traditional Asian ingredient, consisting mostly, as the name strongly implies, of hot chiles and garlic. If, like me, you're a chile-head, you'll find endless ways to use the stuff once you have it on hand. Chilli garlic paste comes in jars, and it keeps for months in the refrigerator. It is worth seeking out at Asian markets or in the international foods aisle of big supermarkets.

- *Chipotle peppers tinned in adobo sauce* – Chipotle peppers are smoked jalapeños. They're very different from regular jalapeños, and they're quite delicious. Look for them, tinned in adobo sauce, in delis, gourmet food shops and online (try www.coolchile.co.uk). Because you're unlikely to use the whole tin at once, you'll be happy to know that you can store your chipotles in the freezer, where they'll keep for months. I just float my tin in a bowl of hot tap water for 5 minutes till it's thawed enough to peel off one or two peppers, then put it right back in the freezer.

- *Fish sauce or nam pla* – This is a salty, fermented seasoning widely used in Southeast Asian cooking, available in Asian supermarkets and in the Asian food sections of big supermarkets. Grab it when you find it; it keeps nicely without refrigeration. Fish sauce is used in a few (really great) recipes in this book, and it adds an authentic flavour. In a pinch, you can substitute soy sauce, although you'll lose some of the Southeast Asian accent.

- *Garlic* – I use only fresh garlic, except for occasional recipes for sprinkle-on seasoning blends. Nothing tastes like the real thing. To my taste buds, even the jarred, chopped garlic in oil doesn't taste like fresh garlic. We won't even *talk* about garlic powder. You may use jarred garlic if you like – half a tsp should equal about 1 clove of fresh garlic. If you choose to use powdered garlic, well, I can't stop you, but I'm afraid I can't promise the recipes will taste the same either. One quarter tsp of garlic powder is the rough equivalent of 1 clove of fresh garlic.

- **Ginger root** – Many recipes in this book call for fresh ginger, sometimes called ginger root. Dried, powdered ginger is *not* a substitute. Fortunately, fresh ginger freezes beautifully. Drop the whole ginger root (called a hand of ginger) into a resealable plastic freezer bag, and toss it in the freezer. When time comes to use it, pull it out, peel enough of the end for your immediate purposes, and grate it. Ginger grates just fine while still frozen. Throw the remaining root back in the bag and toss it back in the freezer.

  Ground fresh ginger root in oil is available in jars at some very comprehensive supermarkets. I buy this when I can find it without added sugar, but otherwise, I grate my own.

- **Guar and xanthan gums** – These sound just dreadful, don't they? But they're in lots of your favourite processed foods, so how bad can they be? They're forms of water-soluble fibre, extracted and purified. Guar and xanthan are both flavourless white powders, and their value to us is as low-carb thickeners. Technically speaking, these are carbs, but they're all fibre. Nothing but.

  Those of you who read *500 Low-Carb Recipes* know that I used to recommend putting your guar or xanthan through the blender with part or all of the liquid in the recipe, to avoid lumps. You may now happily forget that technique. Instead, acquire an extra salt shaker, fill it with guar or xanthan, and keep it handy. When you want to thicken the liquid in your slow cooker, simply sprinkle a little of the thickener over the surface *while stirring*, preferably with a whisk. Stop when your sauce, soup, or gravy is a little less thick than you want it to be. It'll thicken a little more on standing.

  Your health food shop may well be able to order guar or xanthan for you if they don't have them on hand. You can also find suppliers online. Of the two, I slightly prefer xanthan.

- **Ketatoes** – Ketatoes is a low-carb version of instant mashed potatoes. It actually contains some dehydrated potato, diluted with a lot of fibre. You simply mix the powder with equal amounts of water.

  Or not. Personally, I find Ketatoes made according to the pack directions unappealing. They smell good, but the texture is off. However, used in small quantities, Ketatoes mix allows us to give a convincingly potato flavour to a variety of dishes. I've used Ketatoes mix in a number of the recipes in this book. Be aware that Ketatoes come in a variety of flavours, but all my recipes call for Ketatoes Classic – plain potato flavour.

If you can't buy Ketatoes in your hometown, there are about a billion online merchants who would be happy to ship them to you.

- **Low-carb tortillas** – These are becoming easier and easier to find. I can get them at every supermarket in town. If you can't buy them at a local shop, you can order them online. They keep pretty well. I've had them hang around for 3 or 4 weeks in a sealed bag without getting mouldy or stale, so you might want to order more than one pack at a time.

  Beware: I have recently seen 'low-carb' tortillas with deceptive packaging. The listed serving size turned out to equal only half of one tortilla. That's not a serving, as far as I'm concerned!

- **Low-sugar preserves** – In particular, I find low-sugar apricot preserves to be a wonderfully versatile ingredient. This is lower in sugar by *far* than the 'all fruit' preserves, which replace sugar with concentrated fruit juice. Folks, sugar from fruit juice is still sugar. I also have been known to use low-sugar orange marmalade and low-sugar raspberry preserves.

- **Splenda** – Be aware that Splenda granular that comes in bulk, in a box, or in the new 'baker's bag' is different than the Splenda that comes in the little packets. The Splenda in the packets is considerably sweeter. One packet equals 2 tsps granular Splenda. All these recipes use granular Splenda.

- **Sugar-free imitation honey** – This is a polyol (sugar alcohol) syrup with flavouring added to make it taste like honey.

  Sugar-free imitation honey is becoming more and more available, and it is a useful product. Many of the low-carb e-tailers carry Steele's brand of imitation honey. It shouldn't be too hard to get your hands on some.

- **Sugar-free pancake syrup** – This is actually easy to find. All my local supermarkets carry it – indeed, many have more than one brand. It's usually with the regular pancake syrup, but it may be shelved with the diabetic or diet foods. It's just like regular pancake syrup, only it's made from polyols (sugar alcohols) instead of sugar. I use it in small quantities in a few recipes to get a maple flavour.

- **Vege-Sal** – If you've read my newsletter, *Lowcarbezine!* or my previous cookbooks, you know that I'm a big fan of Vege-Sal. It's a salt that's been seasoned, but don't think 'seasoned salt.' Vege-Sal is much milder than traditional seasoned salt. It's simply salt that's been blended with some dried, powdered vegetables. The flavour is quite subtle, but I think it improves all sorts of things. I've given you the choice between using regular salt or Vege-Sal in many recipes. Don't worry, they'll come out fine with plain old salt, but I do think Vege-Sal adds a little something extra. Vege-Sal is made by Modern Products, and it is widely available in health food shops.

CHAPTER ONE

Slow Cooker Snacks and Hot Hors d'oeuvres

Slow cookers are mostly used for cooking dinner while you're out of the house, but they have other uses, such as keeping hors d'oeuvres and dips hot through your whole party! Plus your slow cooker will do the best job of roasting nuts ever. Here are some ways you can make your slow cooker the life of the party.

Glazed Chicken Wings

Put out a pot of these and a big ol' pile of napkins and watch your guests eat!

> 1.5kg chicken wings
> 170g sugar-free imitation honey
> 12g Splenda
> 120ml soy sauce
> 2 tbsp (28ml) oil
> 2 cloves garlic
> 2 tbsp (15g) Dana's No-Sugar Ketchup (see recipe page 228)
>   or purchased low-carb ketchup

Cut the chicken wings in half at the joint. Season them with salt and pepper and put them in your slow cooker.

In a bowl, stir together the honey, Splenda, soy sauce, oil, garlic, and ketchup. Drizzle the mixture over the wings and stir them to coat. Cover the slow cooker, set it to low, and let it cook for 6 to 8 hours.

YIELD: 8 servings, each with: 144 calories, 10g fat, 10g protein, 2g carbohydrate, trace dietary fibre, 2g usable carbs. (Counts do not include the polyols in the imitation honey.)

🍲 Cranberry-Barbeque Meatballs

Boring old ground turkey does a Cinderella turn and comes to the party in this dish!

> 1kg ground turkey
> 2 eggs
> 4 spring onions, finely chopped
> 2 tbsp (28ml) soy sauce
> 1/4 tsp orange extract
> 1/2 tsp pepper
> 1 tsp Splenda
> 60ml oil
> 235ml low-carb barbeque sauce (see recipe page 231 or purchase)
> 110g cranberries (These are strictly seasonal, but they freeze well.)
> 6g Splenda

In a big mixing bowl, combine the turkey, eggs, and spring onions.

In another bowl, mix together the soy sauce, orange extract, pepper, and 1 tsp Splenda and pour into the bowl with the turkey. Now use clean hands to smoosh it all together until it's very well blended. Make 25mm meatballs from the mixture.

Heat half the oil in a big, heavy skillet over medium heat. Brown the meatballs in a few batches, adding the rest of the oil as needed. Transfer the browned meatballs to your slow cooker.

In a blender or food processor with an S-blade, combine the barbeque sauce, cranberries, and the Splenda. Run it until the berries are pureed. Pour this mixture over the meatballs. Cover the slow cooker, set to low, and let it cook for 5 to 6 hours. Serve hot from the slow cooker with toothpicks for spearing!

YIELD: 48 meatballs, each with: 44 calories, 3g fat, 4g protein, 1g carbohydrate, trace dietary fibre, 1g usable carbs.

⊡ Colombo Meatballs with Jerk Sauce

Colombo is the Caribbean version of curry, and jerk is the notoriously fiery barbeque marinade from Jamaica. The heat of this recipe is best controlled by choosing your hot sauce wisely. Use Tabasco, or Louisiana hot sauce, and they'll be spicy. Use Jamaican Scotch Bonnet sauce, or habanero sauce, and they'll take the top of your head right off!

> 455g ground lamb
> 1 egg
> 80g finely chopped onion
> 1/4 tsp ground coriander
> 1/4 tsp ground turmeric
> 1/8 tsp anise seed, ground
> 1 clove garlic, finely chopped
> 1/4 tsp dry mustard
> 2 tsps lemon juice
> 1/2 tsp Splenda
> 1/2 tsp salt
> 2 tbsps (28ml) olive oil
> 1 bay leaf
> 1 tsp ground allspice
> 1 tbsp (8g) grated ginger root
> 1 tbsp (14ml) soy sauce
> 1/4 tsp dried thyme
> 1/4 tsp ground cinnamon
> 1 tbsp (1.5g) Splenda
> 2 cloves garlic, crushed
> 60g low-carb ketchup
> 1 tbsp (15ml) lemon juice
> 1 tbsp (15ml) lime juice
> 1 1/2 tsps hot sauce

In a big mixing bowl, add the lamb, egg, half the finely chopped onion, coriander, turmeric, anise seed, finely chopped garlic, dry mustard, 2 tsps lemon juice, 1/2 tsp Splenda, and salt. Using clean hands, moosh it all together till it's well blended. Then make 25mm meatballs, pressing them together firmly.

Heat the oil in a big, heavy skillet over medium heat and brown the meatballs in two batches. Drop the bay leaf in the bottom of the slow cooker, then put the meatballs on top of it.

Mix together the other half of the finely chopped onion, the allspice, ginger, soy sauce, thyme, cinnamon, 1 tbsp Splenda, crushed garlic, ketchup, 1 tbsp lemon juice, lime juice, and hot sauce. Pour this sauce evenly over the meatballs. Cover the slow cooker, set it to low, and let it cook for 3 hours. Serve hot from the slow cooker.

YIELD: 35 servings, each with: 48 calories, 4g fat, 2g protein, 1g carbohydrate, trace dietary fibre, 1g usable carbs.

Easy Party Shrimp

How easy is this?! Yet your guests will devour it.

> 1 envelope (85g) spicy fish seasoning
>   (try online if your supermarket doesn't stock this)
> 355ml light beer
> 1 tbsp (18g) salt or Vege-Sal
> 2kg easy-peel shrimp or frozen shrimp, unthawed

Drop the spicy fish seasoning net bag into your slow cooker and pour in the beer. (Wrap the seasoning in muslin and secure with thread if is not sold ready-bagged) Add the salt or Vege-Sal and stir. Add the shrimp. Add just enough water to bring the liquid level up to the top of the shrimp. Cover the slow cooker, set it to high, and let it cook for 1 to 2 hours, until the shrimp are pink through. Set the pot to low.

Serve the shrimp straight from the slow cooker with low-carb cocktail sauce, lemon butter, or mustard and mayo stirred together, for dipping. Or if you like, all three! This is enough shrimp for a good-sized party, at least 15 or 20 people, if you're serving it as an hors d'oeuvre/party snack.

YIELD: 20 servings, each with: 101 calories, 2g fat, 18g protein, 1g carbohydrate, 0g dietary fibre, 1g usable carbs. (Analysis does not include any dipping sauces.)

Zippy Cocktail Dogs

Here's an easy way to jazz up those little frankfurters.

60g Dana's No-Sugar Ketchup (see recipe page 228)
  or purchased low-carb ketchup
6g Splenda
1/2 tsp black treacle
1 tsp Worcestershire sauce
60ml bourbon
225g cocktail-size frankfurters

In a large bowl, stir together the ketchup, Splenda, treacle, Worcestershire sauce, and bourbon.

Put the frankfurters in the slow cooker and pour the sauce over them. Cover the slow cooker, set it to low, and let it cook for 2 hours, then uncover and cook for 1 more hour. Serve with toothpicks for spearing.

NOTE: If you can't get cocktail-size frankfurters, use regular frankfurters cut in chunks. They're not as cute, but they should taste the same!

YIELD: 6 servings, each with: 158 calories, 11g fat, 5g protein, 4g carbohydrate, trace dietary fibre, 4g usable carbs.

Horseradish Smokies

My husband loved these!

> 455g small smoked sausage links
> 60g Dana's No-Sugar Ketchup (see recipe page 228)
>   or purchased low-carb ketchup
> 8g Splenda
> 30g prepared horseradish
> 1/4 tsp black treacle

Put the sausages in your slow cooker.

In a bowl, mix the ketchup, Splenda, horseradish, and treacle. Pour the sauce over the sausage. Stir to coat the sausage. Cover the slow cooker, set it to low, and let it cook for 3 hours. Serve the sausage hot from the slow cooker with toothpicks for spearing.

YIELD: 8 servings, each with: 193 calories, 17g fat, 8g protein, 1g carbohydrate, trace dietary fibre, 1g usable carbs.

Orange Smokies

Put these out at your next footie party and watch people eat!

> 450g small smoked sausage links
> 60g Dana's No-Sugar Ketchup (see recipe page 228)
>   or purchased low-carb ketchup
> 60ml lemon juice
> 2 tbsps (3g) Splenda
> 1/4 tsp orange extract
> 1/4 tsp guar or xanthan (optional)

Put the sausages in your slow cooker.

In a small bowl, stir together the ketchup, lemon juice, Splenda, and orange extract. Thicken the mixture just a little, if you think it needs it, with guar or xanthan. Pour the sauce over the sausage. Cover the slow cooker, set it to low, and let it cook for 3 hours. Keep the sausages hot in the slow cooker to serve.

YIELD: 8 servings, each with: 193 calories, 17g fat, 8g protein, 1g carbohydrate, trace dietary fibre, 1g usable carbs.

⌂ Bacon-Cheese Dip

Bacon and cheese together. Just makes you glad to be a low-carber, doesn't it?

    455g softened, or light or regular cream cheese
    225g grated cheddar cheese
    230g Gouda or grated mild, semi-soft cheese
    120ml semi-skimmed milk
    120ml double cream
    2 tbsps (30g) brown mustard
    1 tbsp (10g) finely chopped onion
    2 tsps Worcestershire sauce
    1/2 tsp salt or Vege-Sal
    1/4 tsp cayenne
    455g bacon, cooked, drained, and crumbled

Cut the cream cheese in cubes and put them in your slow cooker. Add the cheddar cheese, the Gouda, milk, cream, mustard, onion, Worcestershire sauce, salt or Vege-Sal, and cayenne. Stir to distribute the ingredients evenly. Cover the slow cooker, set it to low, and let it cook for 1 hour, stirring from time to time.

When the cheese has melted, stir in the bacon.

NOTE: Serve with cut-up vegetables, fibre crackers, or other low-carb dippers.

YIELD: 12 servings, each with: 505 calories, 44g fat, 25g protein, 2g carbohydrate, trace dietary fibre, 2g usable carbs.

◎ Bagna Cauda

The name of this traditional Italian dip means 'hot bath,' and that's just what it is – a bath of hot, flavoured olive oil to dip your vegetables in. Believe it or not, our tester Maria Vander Vloedt's kids really liked this!

235ml extra-virgin olive oil
55g butter
3 cloves garlic, finely chopped
55g tinned anchovies, finely chopped

Combine everything in a small slow cooker. Cover the slow cooker, set it to low, and let it cook for 1 hour.

NOTE: Serve with vegetables. Fennel, pepper strips, cauliflower, mushrooms, celery, tinned artichoke hearts, and lightly steamed asparagus are all traditional choices.

YIELD: Per batch: 2448 calories, 267g fat, 17g protein, 3g carbohydrate, trace dietary fibre, 3g usable carbs. (It's hard to know how to divide this into servings, and it's unlikely you'll end up eating it all, even with a big group. After all, you can't scoop up a tbsp at a time of hot olive oil. So here's the stats for the whole potful. Notice that carb count!)

Hot Artichoke Dip

This is my slow cooker version of the ubiquitous hot artichoke dip that appeared in *500 Low-Carb Recipes*. Using a slow cooker, the dip stays hot till it's gone!

225g mayonnaise
100g grated Parmesan cheese
1 clove garlic, crushed
225g grated mozzarella cheese
400g tinned artichoke hearts, drained and chopped

Add everything to your slow cooker, stir it up well, and smooth the surface. Cover the slow cooker, set it to low, and let it cook for 2 to 3 hours.

Serve with low-carb crackers and/or cut-up vegetables.

YIELD: 8 servings, each with: 339 calories, 33g fat, 11g protein, 2g carbohydrate, 1g dietary fibre, 1g usable carbs.

Hot Crab Dip

Hot crab, hot cheese, garlic – what's not to like?

225g mayonnaise
225g grated cheddar cheese
4 spring onions, finely chopped
170g tinned crabmeat, drained
1 clove garlic, crushed
85g cream cheese, softened, cut into chunks

Combine everything in your slow cooker and stir together. Cover the slow cooker, set it to low, and let it cook for 1 hour. Remove the lid and stir to blend in the now-melted cream cheese. Re-cover and cook for another hour.

Serve with celery, pepper, and cucumber dippers

YIELD: 8 servings, each with: 372 calories, 37g fat, 13g protein, 1g carbohydrate, trace dietary fibre, 1g usable carbs.

⛾ Artichoke-Spinach-Ranch Dip

Artichoke dip, spinach dip, and ranch dip are all so popular, combining them seemed destined for greatness!

400g tinned artichoke hearts, drained and chopped

280g pack frozen chopped spinach, thawed and drained

225g mayonnaise

230g sour cream

1 packet (28g) ranch-style dressing mix

160g grated Parmesan cheese

1 clove garlic, crushed

Spray your slow cooker with oil to prevent sticking. Mix everything together in your slow cooker. Cover, set it to low, and let it cook for 3 to 4 hours. Keep the dip hot in the slow cooker to serve.

NOTE: Serve dip with cut-up vegetables or low-carb crackers.

YIELD: 12 servings, each with: 247 calories, 23g fat, 7g protein, 4g carbohydrate, 1g dietary fibre, 3g usable carbs.

⌢⌣ Chicken Liver Pâté

If you like chicken livers, you'll like this, but you won't if you don't. I adore them myself and practically lived on pâté on fibre crackers for a few days after making this. You could also stuff this into celery stalks.

> 65g finely chopped onion
> 1 clove garlic, crushed
> 100g sliced mushrooms
> 45g butter
> 450g chicken livers
> 2 tbsps (30ml) double cream
> 2 tbsps (30ml) brandy
> 1 bay leaf, crumbled
> 1/2 tsp dried thyme
> 1/2 tsp dried marjoram
> 1 tbsp (4g) chopped fresh parsley
> 3/4 tsp salt or Vege-Sal
> 1/2 tsp pepper

In a big, heavy skillet, start the onion, garlic, and mushrooms sautéing in the butter over low heat. While that's happening, halve the chicken livers where they naturally divide into two lobes. When the mushrooms have softened and changed colour, add the livers and sauté, stirring occasionally, until they're sealed all over and the colour of the surface has changed, but they are not cooked through. Transfer the mixture to a food processor with the S-blade in place.

Add the cream, brandy, bay leaf, thyme, marjoram, parsley, salt or Vege-Sal, and pepper. Run the food processor until the mixture is finely pureed.

Spray a 1 litre glass casserole dish with nonstick cooking spray. Pour the mixture from the food processor into the casserole dish. Place the casserole dish in your slow cooker. Carefully pour water around the casserole dish to within an inch of the rim. Cover the slow cooker, set it to low, and let it cook for 8 hours, or until the mixture is well set. Turn off the slow cooker and let the water cool until you can remove the casserole dish without risk of scalding your fingers. Remove the casserole dish and chill the pâté overnight before serving.

You can simply scoop this from the casserole dish with a knife and spread it on fibre crackers if you like, but it's fancier to turn it out, slice it, and serve it on a bed of greens.

YIELD: 8 servings, each with: 138 calories, 8g fat, 11g protein, 4g carbohydrate, trace dietary fibre, 4g usable carbs.

Roasted Nuts and Seeds

I was astounded by how great a job my slow cooker did of roasting nuts! I got a little carried away, I confess. But then, I really like nuts! Make these often and keep them on hand, and you'll find yourself missing both chips and candy a whole lot less.

⊙ Dana's Snack Mix, Slow Cooker–Style

This is similar to a snack mix that appears in *500 Low-Carb Recipes*, and it's addictive. Thank goodness it's also healthy! You'll likely find shelled pumpkin seeds and raw, shelled sunflower seeds at your health food shop. You can also find the pumpkin seeds in Latino groceries, labeled 'pepitas'.

> 55g butter, melted
> 3 tbsps (50g) Worcestershire sauce
> 1 1/2 tsps garlic powder
> 2 1/2 tsps seasoned salt
> 2 tsps onion powder
> 450g raw pumpkin seeds, shelled
> 225g raw sunflower seeds, shelled
> 145g raw almonds
> 100g raw pecans
> 125g raw walnut pieces
> 130g raw cashews
> 145g dry-roasted peanuts

If you've got a little time, you can just put the butter in the slow cooker, turn it to low, and wait for it to melt. Otherwise, melt it on the stove or in the microwave, and then transfer it to the slow cooker pot. Add the Worcestershire sauce, garlic powder, seasoned salt, and onion powder. Stir it all together. Add the nuts and seeds. Stir well, until all the nuts are evenly coated. Cover the slow cooker, set it to low, and let it cook for 5 to 6 hours, stirring once or twice if you're around.

Uncover the pot, stir the nut and seed mix around, and cook for another 45 to 60 minutes to dry the nuts and seeds. Let them cool before storing them in an airtight container.

YIELD: 24 servings of 50g, each with: 279 calories, 25g fat, 9g protein, 9g carbohydrate, 3g dietary fibre, 6g usable carbs.

Blue Cheese Dressing Walnuts

I originally wanted to make these with powdered blue cheese dressing mix, only to find that there is no such thing, at least not in my supermarkets. So I tried using liquid dressing instead. It didn't end up tasting a lot like blue cheese, but it did end up tasting really good.

> 400g walnuts
> 120ml blue cheese salad dressing
> 1 tsp garlic salt

Combine the walnuts and dressing in your slow cooker. Stir until the nuts are evenly coated with the dressing. Cover the slow cooker, set it to low, and let it cook for 3 hours, stirring once halfway through.

Stir in the garlic salt just before serving.

YIELD: 16 servings, each with: 228 calories, 22g fat, 8g protein, 4g carbohydrate, 2g dietary fibre, 2g usable carbs.

Cajun-Spiced Pecans

You can used purchased Cajun seasoning for this or make your own from the recipe on page 235.

> 455g pecan halves
> 30g butter, melted
> 20g Cajun seasoning

Place the pecans in your slow cooker. Stir in the butter to coat the pecans. Add the Cajun seasoning and stir again to coat. Cover the slow cooker, set it to low, and let it cook for 3 hours, stirring once halfway through if you are around.

YIELD: 16 servings, each with: 118 calories, 12g fat, 1g protein, 4g carbohydrate, 1g dietary fibre, 3g usable carbs.

🝖 Candied Pecans

These are a great treat to leave around in pretty little dishes at a holiday party.

  100g pecan halves
  110g butter, melted
  12g Splenda
  1 1/2 tsps ground cinnamon
  1/4 tsp ground ginger
  1/4 tsp ground allspice

Put the pecans in your slow cooker and stir in the melted butter, coating the pecans thoroughly. Sprinkle the Splenda, cinnamon, ginger, and allspice over the pecans and stir again to coat.

Cover the slow cooker, set it to high, let it cook for 30 minutes. Then uncover, turn it to low, and let it cook for 1 1/2 to 2 hours.

YIELD: 8 servings, each with: 304 calories, 32g fat, 2g protein, 6g carbohydrate, 3g dietary fibre, 3g usable carbs.

⛁ Kickin' Pecans

This isn't enough cayenne to be really hot, just enough to add a little kick. Hence the name.

> 300g pecan halves
> 1 egg white
> 1 tsp cinnamon
> 1/2 tsp salt
> 1/4 tsp cayenne, or more to taste
> 25g Splenda

Put the pecans in your slow cooker. Add the egg white and stir until the pecans are evenly coated.

In a bowl, stir together the cinnamon, salt, cayenne, and Splenda. Pour the mixture over the pecans and stir until they're evenly coated. Cover the slow cooker, set it to low, and let it cook for 3 hours, stirring every hour or so.

If the nuts aren't dry by the end of the 3 hours, uncover the slow cooker, stir, and cook for another 30 minutes until dry. Store in an airtight container.

YIELD: 9 servings, each with: 242 calories, 24g fat, 3g protein, 7g carbohydrate, 3g dietary fibre, 4g usable carbs.

Curried Pecans

These are astonishingly good. I may make them in quantity and give them away for Christmas this year!

45g butter
1/4 tsp black treacle
1 1/2 tsps curry powder
1/4 tsp salt
1/4 tsp ground cumin
350g pecan halves
2 tbsps (3g) Splenda

In a big, heavy skillet, melt the butter over medium-low heat. Stir in the treacle, curry powder, salt, and cumin and cook for just a minute or two.

Add the pecans and stir until they're evenly coated with the butter and seasonings. Then transfer them to your slow cooker. Sprinkle the Splenda over the pecans, stirring as you sprinkle, so you coat them evenly. Cover the slow cooker, set it to low, and let it cook for 2 to 3 hours, stirring once or twice during the cooking time.

YIELD: 9 servings, each with: 169 calories, 17g fat, 2g protein, 4g carbohydrate, 2g dietary fibre, 2g usable carbs.

Smokin' Chilli Peanuts

Oh, my goodness. These are hot and crunchy and just too too good.
But they're not for the faint of heart.

50g butter, melted

2 tbsps (15g) chilli powder

1 tbsp (15ml) liquid smoke flavouring

680g jar salted, dry-roasted peanuts

In your slow cooker, combine the butter, chilli powder, and liquid smoke flavouring.
Stir them together well. Add the peanuts and stir them until they're evenly coated with
the butter and the seasonings. Cover the slow cooker, set it to low, and let it cook for
2 to 2 1/2 hours.

Remove the lid, stir, and let cook for another 30 minutes or until the peanuts are dry.
Store 'em in the original jar!

YIELD: 24 servings, each with: 185 calories, 16g fat, 7g protein, 6g carbohydrate,
2g dietary fibre, 4g usable carbs.

Butter-Spice Almonds

440g almonds

30g butter, melted

2 tsps vanilla extract

2 tsps butter-flavoured extract

12g Splenda

1 tsp ground cinnamon

1/4 tsp salt

Put the almonds in your slow cooker.

In a bowl, stir together the butter, vanilla extract, and butter-flavoured extract until
well combined. Pour the mixture over the almonds and stir to coat. Add the Splenda,
cinnamon, and salt and stir to coat again. Cover the slow cooker, set it to low, and let
it cook for 4 to 5 hours, stirring once or twice.

When the time's up, uncover the slow cooker, stir the almonds again, and let them
cook for another 30 to 45 minutes. Store in an airtight container.

YIELD: 6 servings, each with: 457 calories, 41g fat, 14g protein, 15g carbohydrate,
8g dietary fibre, 7g usable carbs.

Maple-Glazed Walnuts

300g walnuts
1 1/2 tsps ground cinnamon
15g butter, melted
1/4 tsp salt
2 tsps vanilla extract
80ml sugar-free pancake syrup
8g Splenda

Put the walnuts in your slow cooker.

In a bowl, mix together the cinnamon, butter, salt, vanilla extract, pancake syrup, and a third of the Splenda. Pour the mixture over the nuts and stir to coat. Cover the slow cooker, set it to low, and let it cook for 2 to 3 hours, stirring every hour or so.

Then uncover the slow cooker and cook, stirring every 20 minutes, until the nuts are almost dry. Stir in the remaining 2 tbsps Splenda, cook for another 20 minutes, then remove from the slow cooker and cool. Store in an airtight container.

YIELD: 9 servings, each with: 268 calories, 25g fat, 10g protein, 6g carbohydrate, 2g dietary fibre, 4g usable carbs.

Slow Cooker Eggs

Eggs cook so quickly, it seems odd to cook them in your slow cooker, but these couple of dishes come out very well.

Maria's Eggs Florentine

Our tester, Maria, came up with this recipe herself.

225g grated cheddar cheese, divided
280g frozen chopped spinach, thawed and drained
225g tinned mushroom, drained
25g chopped onion
6 eggs, beaten
235ml double cream
1 tsp black pepper
1/2 tsp Italian seasoning
1/2 tsp garlic powder

Spray your slow cooker with nonstick cooking spray. Spread 110g of the cheese on the bottom of the slow cooker. Layer the spinach, mushrooms, and onion.

In a bowl, combine the egg, cream, pepper, Italian seasoning, and garlic powder. Pour the mixture into the slow cooker. Top with the remaining 110g cheese. Cover the slow cooker, set it to high, and let it cook for 2 hours, or until the centre is set.

YIELD: 4 servings, each with: 568 calories, 48g fat, 27g protein, 10g carbohydrate, 4g dietary fibre, 6g usable carbs.

🍲 Broccoli-Bacon-Cheshire Quiche

This crustless quiche is wonderful, but feel free to make any quiche recipe you've got, minus the crust, in the same way. For this recipe, I use broccoli cuts that are bigger than chopped broccoli, but smaller than florets, and I think they're ideal.

500g frozen broccoli florets, thawed and coarsely chopped,
    or a bag of broccoli cuts
225g grated Cheshire cheese
6 rashers of cooked bacon
4 eggs
475ml semi-skinned milk
1 tsp salt or Vege-Sal
1 tsp dry mustard
2 tsps prepared horseradish
1/4 tsp pepper

Spray a 1 1/2-litre glass casserole dish with nonstick cooking spray.

Put the broccoli in the bottom of the casserole dish. Spread the cheese evenly on top of the broccoli and crumble the bacon evenly over the cheese.

In a bowl, whisk together the eggs, milk, salt or Vege-Sal, dry mustard, horseradish, and pepper and pour it over the broccoli in the casserole dish.

Place the casserole dish in your slow cooker and carefully pour water around the casserole dish to within an inch of the rim. Cover the slow cooker, set it to low, and let it cook for 4 hours.

Then turn off the slow cooker, uncover it, and let the water cool until you can remove the casserole dish without risk of scalding your fingers. Serve hot or at room temperature.

YIELD: 6 servings, each with: 292 calories, 21g fat, 20g protein, 6g carbohydrate, 2g dietary fibre, 4g usable carbs.

CHAPTER THREE

Slow Cooker Poultry

Here you will find roughly a billion ways to fix chicken, and some ideas for turkey, too! You'll notice that many (but not all) of these recipes call for the poultry to be skinless. This is because the skin usually doesn't end up very tasty or interesting when moist-cooked as it is in a slow cooker.

I've often specified light meat or dark meat – breasts versus thighs. This is just what appealed to me. Feel free to use whichever you like best, or what's on sale. Often it's cheapest to buy a whole cut-up chicken and strip the skin off yourself at home. That's fine, too – just remove any obvious globs of fat, so your sauce doesn't end up greasy.

⏲ Chicken Burritos

Wow. This is easy, delicious, low-carb, low-calorie, and reheats easily.
What more do you want from a recipe?

> 1.25kg boneless, skinless chicken thighs
> 5 cloves garlic, crushed
> 2 tbsps (15g) chilli powder
> 2 tbsps (30ml) olive oil
> 2 tbsps (30ml) lime juice
> 1 tsp salt
> 1 large jalapeño, finely chopped, or 2 tsps tinned jalapeños
> 12 low-carb tortillas
> 70g shredded lettuce
> 110g grated cheddar cheese
> 180g light sour cream
> 195g salsa
> 10g chopped fresh coriander (optional)

Place the chicken in your slow cooker.

In a bowl, mix the garlic, chilli powder, oil, lime juice, salt, and jalapeño together.
Pour over the chicken and stir to coat. Cover the slow cooker, set it to low, and let
it cook for 10 hours. (Or cook on high for 5 hours.)

When the time's up, stir the mixture with a fork to reduce the chicken to a big pot
of tasty chicken shreds. Fill each tortilla with 75g chicken and top with lettuce, cheese,
1 tbsp sour cream, a generous tbsp salsa, and a sprinkling of coridander if desired.
Wrap and devour!

This is a great meal for a family that has some low-carbers and some non–low-
carbers, just give them regular or (preferably) whole wheat flour tortillas. The chicken
keeps well in the fridge, and reheats quickly in the microwave for a fast snack. (I find
that 45 seconds on 70 percent power is about right for a single serving.)

YIELD: 12 servings, each with: 225 calories, 13g fat, 22g protein, 14g carbohydrate,
9g dietary fibre, 5g usable carbs.

Seriously Simple Chicken Chilli

The name says it all!

   1kg boneless, skinless chicken breasts
   455g jar prepared salsa
   1 tbsp (7g) chilli powder
   1 tsp chicken bouillon concentrate
   85g grated soft smoked cheese
   90g light sour cream

Put the chicken in your slow cooker.

In a bowl, stir together the salsa, chilli powder, and bouillon, making sure the bouillon's dissolved. Pour the mixture over the chicken. Cover the slow cooker, set it to low, and let it cook for 7 to 8 hours.

When the time's up, shred the chicken with a fork. Serve topped with the cheese and sour cream.

YIELD: 6 servings, each with: 263 calories, 9g fat, 39g protein, 6g carbohydrate, 2g dietary fibre, 4g usable carbs.

⛁ Chicken Chilli Verde

This repeat from *15-Minute Low-Carb Recipes* is marvellous, and it's a really nice change from the traditional beef chilli.

700g boneless, skinless chicken breasts

390g prepared salsa verde

1/2 medium onion, chopped

1 bay leaf

1/2 tsp pepper

1 tsp ground cumin

1 tsp finely chopped garlic or 2 cloves garlic, crushed

1–2 tbsps (6–12g) jarred, sliced jalapeño

    (I use 2 tbsps, and it makes the chilli pretty hot.)

2 tsps chicken bouillon concentrate

Guar or xanthan (optional)

Sour cream

Grated soft smoked cheese

2 tbsp Chopped fresh coriander

Place the chicken in your slow cooker and add the salsa verde, onion, bay leaf, pepper, cumin, garlic, jalapeños, and bouillon on top. Cover the slow cooker, set it to low, and let it cook for 9 to 10 hours.

When the time's up, shred the chicken with a fork. Stir it up, thicken the chilli a little with the guar or xanthan if you think it needs it, and serve with sour cream, cheese, and coriander on top.

YIELD: 5 servings, each with: 190 calories, 2g fat, 32g protein, 7g carbohydrate, trace dietary fibre, 7g usable carbs. (Analysis does not include garnishes.)

⛖ Chicken Cacciatore

Here's a slow cooker version of an old favourite. It's easy, too, what I call a throw-it-together-and-go recipe.

> 6 skinless chicken leg and side quarters (about 1.5kg)
>
> 500g no-sugar-added spaghetti sauce (I use Hunt's.)
>
> 225g whole tinned mushrooms, drained
>
> 2 tsps dried oregano
>
> 50g chopped onion
>
> 1 green bell pepper, diced
>
> 2 cloves garlic, crushed
>
> 60ml dry red wine
>
> Guar or xanthan (optional)

Simply put everything except the guar or xanthan in your slow cooker and stir it up to combine. Cover the slow cooker, set it to low, and let it cook for 7 hours.

When the time's up, remove the chicken with tongs and put it in a big serving bowl. Thicken the sauce up a little with the guar or xanthan if it needs it and ladle the sauce over the chicken.

If you like, you can serve this over Cauli-Rice (page 239), spaghetti squash, or even low-carb pasta, but I'd probably eat it as is.

YIELD: 6 servings, each with: 293 calories, 8g fat, 42g protein, 11g carbohydrate, 4g dietary fibre, 7g usable carbs.

Chicken Paprikash

Hungarian decadence! Feel free to use full-fat sour cream in this sumptuous gravy if you prefer. Or you could use plain yogurt, just drain off any watery whey first.

    50g chopped onion
    15g butter
    1 tbsp (15ml) oil
    1.5kg chicken thighs
    120ml chicken stock
    60ml dry white wine
    1 1/2 tbsps (24g) tomato paste
    1 tsp chicken bouillon concentrate
    1 1/2 tbsps (10g) paprika
    1/2 tsp caraway seeds
    1/4 tsp pepper
    120g light sour cream
    Guar or xanthan (optional)

In a big, heavy skillet, sauté the onion in the butter and oil over medium-low heat, until it's just golden. Transfer it to your slow cooker. Add the chicken to the skillet, turn the heat up to medium, and brown the chicken all over. Transfer it to the slow cooker, too.

Pour off the fat from the skillet and pour in the stock and wine. Stir it around to dissolve the tasty brown stuff stuck to the skillet, then stir in the tomato paste and bouillon. When those are dissolved, pour the liquid over the chicken.

Sprinkle the paprika, caraway seeds, and pepper over the chicken. Cover the slow cooker, set it to low, and let it cook for 6 hours.

When the time's up, remove the chicken with tongs or a slotted spoon and put it on a platter. Whisk the sour cream into the liquid in the slow cooker and thicken it further with guar or xanthan if desired. Serve the sauce with the chicken.

Don't forget to serve this with Fauxtatoes (see recipe page 239) to ladle this beautiful gravy onto!

YIELD: 5 servings, each with: 537 calories, 39g fat, 39g protein, 5g carbohydrate, 1g dietary fibre, 4g usable carbs.

Curried Chicken with Coconut Milk

The day I first made this, my cleaning crew was here, and they couldn't stop talking about how great it smelled. It tastes even better! Find coconut milk in the Asian section of big supermarkets or at Asian markets. It comes in regular or light, and they generally have the same carb count, so choose whichever you prefer.

> 1.5kg skinless chicken thighs
> 50g chopped onion
> 2 cloves garlic, crushed
> 1 1/2 tbsps (10g) curry powder
> 235ml coconut milk
> 1 tsp chicken bouillon concentrate
> Guar or xanthan

Put the chicken in your slow cooker. Place the onion and garlic over it.

In a bowl, mix together the curry powder, coconut milk, and bouillon. Pour the mixture over the chicken and vegetables in the slow cooker. Cover the slow cooker, set it to low, and let it cook for 6 hours.

When the time's up, remove the chicken and put it on a platter. Thicken the sauce to a gravy consistency with guar or xanthan.

You'll want to serve this with Cauli-Rice (see recipe page 239) to soak up the extra curry sauce. It's too good to miss!

YIELD: 5 servings, each with: 310 calories, 18g fat, 32g protein, 6g carbohydrate, 2g dietary fibre, 4g usable carbs.

Chicken Vindaloo

I made this at a local campground over a holiday weekend, and it was a huge hit with fellow campers. It's exotic and wonderful.

3kg boneless, skinless chicken thighs

1 medium onion, chopped

5 cloves garlic, crushed

30g grated ginger root

4 tsps Garam Masala (see recipe page 236) or purchased garam masala

1 tsp ground turmeric

60ml lime juice

60ml rice vinegar

120ml chicken stock

1 tsp salt

Put the chicken, onion, and garlic in your slow cooker.

In a bowl, stir together the ginger, garam masala, turmeric, lime juice, vinegar, stock, and salt. Pour the mixture over the chicken. Cover the slow cooker, set it to low, and let it cook for 6 to 7 hours.

Serve with Slow Cooker Chutney (see recipe page 208).

YIELD: 12 servings, each with: 295 calories, 10g fat, 46g protein, 2g carbohydrate, trace dietary fibre, 2g usable carbs.

Chicken with Raspberry-Chipotle Sauce

Oh goodness, is this wonderful. My only regret about this recipe is that the Raspberry-Chipotle Sauce loses its brilliant ruby colour during the long, slow cooking. But the flavour definitely remains. Consider using this simple sauce uncooked as a condiment on roasted poultry or pork. If you can't find raspberry syrup at a local coffee joint, you can order it online.

> 1.5kg chicken
>
> 6 tsps adobo seasoning (see recipe p236)
>
> 2 tbsps (30ml) oil
>
> 120g raspberries
>
> 60ml raspberry-flavoured sugar-free coffee flavouring syrup
>
> 1 chipotle chilli tinned in adobo sauce (found in delis and gourmet food shops, and online, try www.coolchile.co.uk)
>
> 1 tbsp (14ml) white wine vinegar
>
> 5g chopped fresh coriander (optional)

Sprinkle the chicken all over with the adobo seasoning.

In a big, heavy skillet, heat the oil over medium-high heat, then brown the chicken all over. Transfer the chicken to your slow cooker.

In a blender or food processor with the S-blade in place, combine the raspberries, raspberry-flavoured coffee syrup, chipotle, and vinegar. Process till smooth. Pour the mixture evenly over the chicken. Cover the slow cooker, set it to low, and let it cook for 6 hours.

Stir the sauce before serving it over the chicken. Sprinkle a little coriander over each piece of chicken, if desired.

YIELD: 5 servings, each with: 492 calories, 36g fat, 35g protein, 5g carbohydrate, 2g dietary fibre, 3g usable carbs.

☖ Chicken Stew

This dish is a nice change from the usual beef stew. It's light, flavourful, and your whole meal in one pot.

    2 tbsps (30ml) olive oil
    700g boneless, skinless chicken thighs, cut into 1' cubes
    225g sliced mushrooms
    1 medium onion, sliced
    340g courgette slices
    4 cloves garlic, crushed
    400g tinned tomato wedges
    175ml chicken stock
    1 tsp chicken bouillon concentrate
    1 tbsp (4g) poultry seasoning
    Guar or xanthan

In a big, heavy skillet, heat 1 tbsp of the oil. Brown the chicken until it is golden all over. Transfer the chicken to your slow cooker.

Heat the remaining 1 tbsp of oil in the skillet and sauté the mushrooms, onion, and courgette until the mushrooms change colour and the onions are translucent. Transfer them to the slow cooker, too. Add the garlic and tomatoes to the slow cooker.

Put the stock and bouillon in the skillet and stir them around to dissolve any flavourful bits sticking to the skillet. Pour into the slow cooker. Sprinkle the poultry seasoning over the mixture. Cover the slow cooker, set it to low, and let it cook for 4 to 5 hours.

When the time's up, thicken the liquid in the slow cooker with guar or xanthan.

YIELD: 6 servings, each with: 159 calories, 8g fat, 11g protein, 12g carbohydrate, 2g dietary fibre, 10g usable carbs.

Chicken with Root Vegetables, Cabbage, and Herbs

I think of this as being a sort of French Country dish. Of course, I've never been to the French countryside, so what do I know? It's good, though, and you don't need another single thing with it.

2.5kg chicken

1 1/2 tbsps (20ml) olive oil

20g butter

2 medium turnips, cut into 2cm cubes

2 medium carrots, cut into 2cm slices

1 medium onion, cut into 1cm half-rounds

1 head cabbage

4 cloves garlic, crushed

1/2 tsp dried rosemary

1/2 tsp dried thyme

1/2 tsp dried basil

2 bay leaves, crumbled

In a big, heavy skillet, brown the chicken on both sides in the oil and butter over medium-high heat.

When the chicken is browned all over, remove it to a plate and reserve. Some extra fat will have accumulated in the skillet, pour off all but a couple of tbsps, then add the turnips, carrots, and onion. Sauté them, scraping the tasty brown bits off the bottom of the skillet as you stir, until they're getting a touch of gold, too.

Transfer the sautéed vegetables to your slow cooker.

Cut the cabbage into eighths and put it on top of the vegetables. Arrange the chicken on top of the cabbage. Sprinkle the garlic over the chicken and vegetables, making sure some ends up on the chicken and some down among the vegetables. Sprinkle the rosemary, thyme, basil, and bay leaves into the slow cooker, making sure some gets down into the vegetables. Season with salt and pepper. Cover the slow cooker, set it to low, and let it cook for 6 to 7 hours.

YIELD: 8 servings, each with: 510 calories, 37g fat, 36g protein, 6g carbohydrate, 2g dietary fibre, 4g usable carbs.

⛁ Citrus Spice Chicken

Sunshiny citrus flavour! Another throw-it-together-and-go recipe.

   80ml lemon juice
   2 tbsps (3g) Splenda
   1/2 tsp orange extract
   120g Dana's No-Sugar Ketchup (see recipe page 228)
      or purchased low-carb ketchup
   2 tbsps (40g) low-sugar orange marmalade
   1/2 tsp ground cinnamon
   1/2 tsp ground allspice
   1/8 tsp ground cloves
   1/4 tsp cayenne
   1.5kg skinless chicken thighs

In a bowl, stir together the lemon juice, Splenda, orange extract, ketchup, marmalade, cinnamon, allspice, cloves, and cayenne.

Put the chicken in your slow cooker and pour the sauce over it. Cover the slow cooker, set it to low, and let it cook for 6 hours.

Serve with Cauli-Rice (see recipe page 239).

YIELD: 5 servings, each with: 191 calories, 6g fat, 31g protein, 2g carbohydrate, trace dietary fibre, 2g usable carbs.

Italian Chicken and Vegetables

1/2 head cabbage, cut in wedges

1 medium onion, sliced

225g sliced mushrooms

1kg skinless chicken breasts

1kg skinless chicken thighs

500g no-sugar-added spaghetti sauce

Guar or xanthan (optional)

Grated Parmesan cheese

Put the cabbage, onion, and mushrooms in your slow cooker. Place the chicken on top of the vegetables. Pour the spaghetti sauce over the top.

Cover the slow cooker, set it to low, and let it cook for 6 hours. Thicken the sauce with guar or xanthan if needed and serve with Parmesan cheese.

YIELD: 6 servings, each with: 254 calories, 5g fat, 46g protein, 4g carbohydrate, 1g dietary fibre, 3g usable carbs.

⊡ Lemon Chicken

1.5kg skinless chicken thighs

30g butter

1 tsp dried oregano

1/2 tsp seasoned salt

1/4 tsp pepper

60ml chicken stock

45ml lemon juice

2 cloves garlic, crushed

2 tbsps (8g) chopped fresh parsley

1 tsp chicken bouillon concentrate

Guar or xanthan

In a big, heavy skillet, brown the chicken in the butter over medium-high heat.

In a bowl, mix together the oregano, seasoned salt, and pepper. When the chicken is golden, sprinkle the spice mixture over it. Transfer the chicken to your slow cooker.

Pour the stock and lemon juice in the skillet, stirring around to deglaze the pan. Add the garlic, parsley, and bouillon. Stir until the bouillon dissolves. Pour into the slow cooker.

Cover the slow cooker, set it to low, and let it cook for 4 to 5 hours. When the chicken is tender, remove it from the slow cooker. Thicken the sauce a bit with guar or xanthan. Serve the sauce with the chicken.

This dish goes well with Cauli-Rice (see recipe page 239).

YIELD: 6 servings, each with: 200 calories, 9g fat, 26g protein, 2g carbohydrate, 1g dietary fibre, 1g usable carbs.

Chicken with Thyme and Artichokes

This is sort of classic, yet very little work.

> 700g boneless, skinless chicken thighs
> 2 tbsps (30ml) olive oil
> 120ml dry white wine
> 1 tbsp (15ml) lemon juice
> 1 tsp chicken bouillon concentrate
> 2 tsps dried thyme
> 1 clove garlic, crushed
> 1/4 tsp pepper
> 400g tinned artichoke hearts, drained
> Guar or xanthan

In a big, heavy skillet, brown the chicken in the oil over medium-high heat until golden on both sides. Transfer to your slow cooker.

In a bowl, stir together the wine, lemon juice, bouillon, thyme, garlic, and pepper. Pour the mixture over the chicken. Place the artichokes on top. Cover the slow cooker, set it to low, and let it cook for 6 hours.

Scoop out the chicken and artichokes with a slotted spoon. Thicken the liquid left in the pot with just enough guar or xanthan to make it the thickness of single cream.

Serve the chicken and artichokes, plus the sauce, over Cauli-Rice (see recipe page 239).

YIELD: 4 servings, each with: 314 calories, 10g fat, 42g protein, 7g carbohydrate, trace dietary fibre, 7g usable carbs.

⊙ Lemon–White Wine–Tarragon Chicken

This is similar to the previous recipe, except, of course, that tarragon is very different from thyme and there are no artichokes.

   1.5kg skinless chicken thighs
   120ml dry white wine
   120ml lemon juice
   1 tsp Splenda
   1 tbsp (2g) dried tarragon
   1/2 tsp pepper
   1 tsp chicken bouillon concentrate
   Guar or xanthan

Put the chicken in your slow cooker.

In a bowl, mix together the wine, lemon juice, Splenda, tarragon, pepper, and bouillon, stirring until the bouillon dissolves. Pour the mixture over the chicken. Cover the slow cooker, set it to low, and let it cook for 6 hours.

Remove the chicken to serving plates and thicken the remaining liquid with guar or xanthan to achieve the texture of cream.

YIELD: 6 servings, each with: 176 calories, 5g fat, 26g protein, 3g carbohydrate, trace dietary fibre, 3g usable carbs.

Mum's 1960s Chicken

Back in the 1960s my mum would make a dish for company with chicken breasts, wrapped in bacon, laid on a layer of chipped beef, topped with a sauce made of sour cream and cream of mushroom soup. It tasted far more sophisticated than it sounds and never failed to draw raves from dinner party guests. This is my attempt to de-carb and slow-cooker-ize the same dish – without the carb-filled cream of mushroom soup.

60g dried beef slices (aka 'chipped beef')

6 rashers of bacon

1kg boneless, skinless chicken breasts

100g sliced mushrooms

1 tbsp (15g) butter

235ml double cream

1 tsp beef bouillon concentrate

1 pinch onion powder

1 pinch celery salt

1/4 tsp pepper

Guar or xanthan

230g sour cream

Paprika

Line the bottom of your slow cooker with the dried beef.

Place the bacon in a glass pie plate or on a microwave bacon rack and microwave for 3 to 4 minutes on high. Drain the bacon and reserve. (What you're doing here is cooking some of the grease off of the bacon, without cooking it to a crisp.)

Cut the chicken into 6 servings. Wrap each piece of chicken in a slice of bacon and place it in the slow cooker on top of the dried beef.

In a big, heavy skillet, sauté the mushrooms in the butter until they're soft. Add the cream and bouillon and stir until the bouillon dissolves. Stir in the onion powder, celery salt, and pepper, then thicken with guar or xanthan until the mixture reaches a gravy consistency. Stir in the sour cream.

Spoon this mixture over the chicken breasts and sprinkle with a little paprika. Cover the slow cooker, set it to low, and let it cook for 5 to 6 hours.

To serve, scoop up some of the dried beef and sauce with each bacon-wrapped piece of chicken.

YIELD: 6 servings, each with: 472 calories, 32g fat, 41g protein, 4g carbohydrate, trace dietary fibre, 4g usable carbs.

🝰 Slow Cooker Chicken Mole

Chicken mole is the national dish of Mexico, and I'm crazy about it. On my honeymoon in Mexico, I bought a container of chicken mole at the deli in the local supermarket and kept it in the hotel room fridge to heat up in the microwave! Here's a slow cooker version.

400g tinned tomatoes with green chillies

50g chopped onion

30g slivered almonds, toasted

3 cloves garlic, crushed

3 tbsps (17g) unsweetened cocoa powder

35g raisins

1 tbsp (7g) sesame seeds

1 tbsp (1.5g) Splenda

1/4 tsp ground cinnamon

1/4 tsp ground nutmeg

1/4 tsp ground coriander

1/4 tsp salt

1.5kg skinless chicken thighs

Guar or xanthan

2 tbsps (15g) slivered almonds, toasted

Put the tomatoes, onion, almonds, garlic, cocoa powder, raisins, sesame seeds, Splenda, cinnamon, nutmeg, coriander, and salt in a blender or food processor and puree coarsely.

Place the chicken in your slow cooker. Pour the sauce over it. Cover the slow cooker, set it to low, and let it cook for 9 to 10 hours.

Remove the chicken from the slow cooker with tongs. Thicken the sauce to taste with guar or xanthan. Serve the sauce over the chicken. Top with the 2 tbsps almonds.

YIELD: 8 servings, each with: 284 calories, 12g fat, 37g protein, 8g carbohydrate, 2g dietary fibre, 6g usable carbs.

⬚ Mediterranean Chicken

This recipe, bursting with classic Mediterranean flavours, originally appeared in *500 More Low-Carb Recipes*.

   225g sliced mushrooms
   400g tinned tomatoes
   170g tinned artichoke hearts
   70g sliced black olives
   1.5kg skinless chicken thighs
   1 tbsp (4g) Italian seasoning
   175ml chicken stock
   1 tsp chicken bouillon concentrate
   60ml dry white wine
   Guar or xanthan

Put the mushrooms, tomatoes, artichokes, and olives in your slow cooker. Place the chicken on top.

In a bowl, mix together the Italian seasoning, stock, bouillon, and wine. Pour the sauce over the chicken and vegetables. Cover the slow cooker, set it to low, and let it cook for 7 hours.

When the time's up, thicken the juices a bit with guar or xanthan.

YIELD: 6 servings, each with: 215 calories, 7g fat, 28g protein, 8g carbohydrate, 2g dietary fibre, 6g usable carbs.

⛁ Orange Teriyaki Chicken

This has been officially rated 'Very Easy, Very Good!'

450g frozen Oriental vegetable mixture, unthawed

1kg boneless, skinless chicken breasts, cubed

175ml chicken stock

2 tbsps (35g) Low-Carb Teriyaki Sauce (see recipe p233)
    or purchased low-carb teriyaki sauce

1 tsp chicken bouillon concentrate

1 tbsp (20g) low-sugar orange marmalade

1/4 tsp orange extract

2 tbsps (30ml) lemon juice

1 tsp Splenda

1 tsp dry mustard

1/2 tsp ground ginger

Guar or xanthan

Pour the vegetables into your slow cooker. Place the chicken on top.

In a bowl, combine the stock, teriyaki sauce, bouillon, marmalade, orange extract, lemon juice, Splenda, dry mustard, and ginger, stirring well. Pour the mixture over the chicken and veggies. Cover the slower cooker, set it to low, and let it cook for 4 to 5 hours.

Before serving, thicken the sauce a bit with guar or xanthan.

Serve over Cauli-Rice (see recipe page 239) if desired. Or for the carbivores you can serve it over brown rice, lo mein noodles, or plain old spaghetti.

YIELD: 6 servings, each with: 222 calories, 4g fat, 36g protein, 7g carbohydrate, 2g dietary fibre, 5g usable carbs.

⊙ Thai Chicken Bowls

This was a big hit with Maria's family!

8 boneless, skinless, boneless chicken thighs, cubed (a little over 1 kg)

2 cloves garlic, crushed

50g chopped onion

2 stalks celery, sliced

2 tsps grated ginger root

1 tsp five-spice powder

1/2 tsp salt

1 tbsp (15ml) lemon juice

1 tsp hot sauce (optional)

850ml chicken stock

1 head cauliflower

Guar or xanthan

6 tbsps (35g) sliced spring onions

6 tbsps (7g) chopped coriander

Place the chicken in your slow cooker. Top with the garlic, onion, celery, ginger, five-spice powder, salt, and lemon juice.

In a bowl, combine the hot sauce, if using, with the stock and pour it into the slow cooker. Cover the slow cooker, set it to low, and let it cook for 5 to 6 hours.

Okay, it's almost supper time. Run your cauliflower through the shredding blade of your food processor to make Cauli-Rice. Put your Cauli-Rice in a microwaveable casserole with a lid, add a couple of tbsps of water, cover, and microwave on high for 6 minutes.

Thicken up the sauce in the slow cooker with a little guar or xanthan to about the texture of double cream.

Okay, Cauli-Rice is done! Uncover it immediately, drain, and divide it into 6 bowls. Divide the chicken mixture, ladling it over the Cauli-Rice. Top with the spring onions and coriander.

YIELD: 6 servings, each with: 138 calories, 4g fat, 20g protein, 4g carbohydrate, 1g dietary fibre, 3g usable carbs.

Thai Hot Pot

This recipe takes a few more steps than some, but the results are worth it!
If you can't get Southeast Asian fish sauce, you can substitute soy sauce.

700g boneless, skinless chicken thighs

1 medium carrot, sliced

1 medium onion, sliced

1 clove garlic, crushed

425ml coconut milk

1 tbsp (8g) grated ginger root

2 tbsps (35g) fish sauce (nam pla) or soy sauce

1 tbsp (15ml) lime juice

2 tsps Splenda

1/2 tsp hot sauce

90g natural peanut butter

450g shrimp, shelled

75g fresh mange tout, cut into 2cm pieces

Guar or xanthan

720g Cauli-Rice (see recipe page 239)

60g chopped peanuts

Put the chicken in your slow cooker and add the carrot, onion, and garlic.

In a blender, combine the coconut milk, ginger, fish sauce or soy sauce, lime juice, Splenda, hot sauce, and peanut butter and blend until smooth. Pour the sauce over the chicken and vegetables, using a rubber scraper to make sure you get all of it! Cover the slow cooker, set it to low, and let it cook for 8 hours.

Stir in the shrimp and snow peas, re-cover the slow cooker, and turn it up to high. Cook for 10 minutes, or until the shrimp are pink through.

Thicken the sauce slightly with guar or xanthan. Serve over the Cauli-Rice (or brown rice, for the carb-eaters.) Top each serving with the peanuts.

YIELD: 6 servings, each with: 480 calories, 32g fat, 33g protein, 19g carbohydrate, 7g dietary fibre, 12g usable carbs.

Yassa

This chicken stew comes from Senegal. Traditionally it is quite hot, so feel free to increase the cayenne if you like!

    3 large onions, thinly sliced
    6 cloves garlic, crushed
    120ml lemon juice
    1 1/2 tsps salt
    1/2 tsp cayenne, or more to taste
    3kg chicken, cut up
    60ml oil
    960g Cauli-Rice (see recipe page 239)

In your slow cooker, combine the onions, garlic, lemon juice, salt, and cayenne. Add the chicken and toss, so that all the chicken comes in contact with the seasonings. Cover your slow cooker and refrigerate overnight. (It's a good idea to stir this a few times if you think of it, though I don't expect you to get up in the middle of the night to do it!)

Using tongs, remove the chicken from the marinade. Pat it dry with paper towels and set it aside. Transfer the marinade to your slow cooker.

In a big, heavy skillet, heat the oil over medium-high heat. Place the chicken skin side down, and cook it until the skin is browned. (You'll need to do this in batches, unless your skillet is a lot bigger than mine!) Don't bother browning the other side of the chicken.

Transfer the chicken back to the slow cooker with the marinade. Cover the slow cooker, set it to low, and let it cook for 5 to 6 hours.

Remove the chicken from the slow cooker with tongs. Put the chicken on a platter, cover it with foil, and put it in a warm place.

Ladle the onions and liquid out of the slow cooker into the skillet and turn the heat to high. Boil this hard, stirring often, until most of the liquid has evaporated. (You want the volume reduced by more than half.) Serve the chicken, onions, and sauce over the Cauli-Rice.

YIELD: 8 servings, each with: 638 calories, 46g fat, 45g protein, 11g carbohydrate, 3g dietary fibre, 8g usable carbs.

☺ Southwestern Barbeque

This is incredibly popular, for something so easy!

> 125g tomato sauce
> 1 tbsp (2g) Splenda
> 1 1/2 tbsps (9g) tinned, sliced jalapeños
> 2 tbsps (30ml) lime juice
> 1/8 tsp black treacle
> 1 tsp ground cumin
> 1/4 tsp red pepper flakes
> 2kg skinless chicken thighs

Combine everything except for the chicken in your slow cooker and stir well. Place the chicken in the sauce, meaty side down. Cover the slow cooker, set it to low, and let it cook for 6 hours.

Serve the chicken with the sauce spooned over it.

YIELD: 6 servings, each with: 215 calories, 7g fat, 34g protein, 2g carbohydrate, trace dietary fibre, 2g usable carbs.

⊡ Chicken and Dumplings

This takes some work, but boy, is it comfort food. You could make this with left-over turkey instead if you prefer. If you do that, put the cubed, cooked turkey in about 5 to 6 hours into the initial cooking time.

2 medium carrots, sliced

1 medium onion, in chunks

2 medium turnips, cut into 2cm cubes

225g frozen green beans, cross-cut

225g sliced mushrooms

700g boneless, skinless chicken thighs, cut into 4cm cubes

355ml chicken stock

1 tsp poultry seasoning

3 tsps chicken bouillon concentrate

120ml double cream

Guar or xanthan

Dumplings (see recipe on next page)

In your slow cooker, combine the carrots, onion, turnips, green beans, mushrooms, and chicken.

In a bowl, mix together the stock, poultry seasoning, and bouillon. Pour the mixture over the chicken and vegetables. Cover the slow cooker, set it to low, and let it cook for 6 to 7 hours.

When the time's up, stir in the cream and thicken the gravy to a nice consistency with guar or xanthan. Add salt and pepper to taste. Re-cover the slow cooker and turn it to high.

While the slow cooker is heating up (it'll take at least 30 minutes), make your Dumplings, stopping before you add the liquid. Wait until the gravy in the slow cooker is boiling. Then stir in the buttermilk and drop the biscuit dough by spoonfuls over the surface of the chicken and gravy. Re-cover the slow cooker and let it cook for another 25 to 30 minutes.

YIELD: 8 servings, each with: 417 calories, 25g fat, 36g protein, 14g carbohydrate, 4g dietary fibre, 10g usable carbs. (Calculations include the Dumplings.)

⊙ Dumplings

Feel free to use this with other meat-and-gravy dishes if you like!
(These instructions require gravy to boil the Dumplings in.)

> 110g ground almonds
> 120g rice protein powder (Get this at your health food shop.
>   If they don't have it, they can order it. I use NutriBiotic brand.)
> 30g wheat gluten
> 30g butter
> 2 tbsps (30ml) coconut oil
> 1/2 tsp salt
> 2 tsps baking powder
> 1/2 tsp baking soda
> 180ml buttermilk

Put everything but the buttermilk into your food processor with the S-blade in place. Pulse the food processor to cut in the butter. (You want it evenly distributed in the dry ingredients.) Dump this mixture into a mixing bowl.

Check to make sure your gravy is boiling. (If it isn't, have a quick cup of tea until it is.) Now pour the buttermilk into the dry ingredients and stir it in with a few swift strokes. (Don't over-mix; you just want to make sure everything's evenly damp.) This will make a soft dough. Drop by spoonfuls over the boiling gravy, cover the pot, and let it cook for 25 to 30 minutes.

NOTE: Grind 3/4 cup almonds to cormeal-like consistency, or use almond meal.

YIELD: 12 servings, each with: 153 calories, 10g fat, 14g protein, 4g carbohydrate, 1g dietary fibre, 3g usable carbs.

Chicken in Creamy Horseradish Sauce

Don't think that just because this has horseradish it's really strong. The sauce is mellow, subtle, and family-friendly.

    2kg cut-up chicken
    15g butter
    1 tbsp (15ml) olive oil
    175ml chicken stock
    1 1/2 tsps chicken bouillon concentrate
    1 tbsp (15g) prepared horseradish
    115g cream cheese, cut into chunks
    60ml double cream
    Guar or xanthan (optional)

In a big, heavy skillet, brown the chicken in the butter and oil over medium-high heat. Transfer the chicken to your slow cooker.

In a bowl, stir together the stock, bouillon, and horseradish. Pour the mixture over the chicken. Cover the slow cooker, set it to low, and let it cook for 6 hours.

When the time's up, remove the chicken with tongs and put it on a platter. Melt the cream cheese into the sauce in the slow cooker. Stir in the cream. Thicken the sauce with guar or xanthan if you think it needs it. Add salt and pepper to taste.

I think this would be good with Fauxtatoes (see recipe page 239) and green beans.

YIELD: 8 servings, each with: 442 calories, 34g fat, 30g protein, 1g carbohydrate, trace dietary fibre, 1g usable carbs.

Chicken in Creamy Orange Sauce

2kg skinless chicken thighs

3 tbsps (45ml) oil

3 tbsps (45ml) brandy

120ml white wine vinegar

120ml lemon juice

$1/2$ tsp orange extract

1 tsp grated orange rind

8g Splenda

8 spring onions, sliced

170g light cream cheese, cut into chunks

Guar or xanthan (optional)

In a big, heavy skillet, brown the chicken in the oil over medium-high heat. Transfer the chicken to your slow cooker.

In a bowl, stir together the brandy, vinegar, lemon juice, orange extract, and Splenda. Pour the mixture over chicken. Cover the slow cooker, set it to low, and let it cook for 6 hours.

When the time's up, transfer the chicken to a platter. Add the spring onions to the liquid in the slow cooker, then add the cream cheese and stir till it's melted. Thicken with guar or xanthan if you think it needs it. Add salt and pepper to taste. Serve the sauce over the chicken.

Cauli-Rice (see recipe page 239) in one form or another is the natural side dish with this. Add a big green salad, and there's supper!

YIELD: 8 servings, each with: 359 calories, 20g fat, 35g protein, 5g carbohydrate, trace dietary fibre, 5g usable carbs.

Tuscan Chicken

This is fabulous Italian chicken!

2kg skinless chicken thighs

1 tbsp (15ml) olive oil

50g chopped onion

1 red bell pepper, cut into strips

1 green bell pepper, cut into strips

425g tinned black soybeans, drained

410g tinned crushed tomatoes

120ml dry white wine

1 tsp dried oregano

1 clove garlic, crushed

1 tsp chicken bouillon concentrate

In a big, heavy skillet, brown the chicken in the oil over medium-high heat.

Meanwhile, put the onion, peppers, and soybeans in your slow cooker. Place the chicken on top of the vegetables and beans.

In a bowl, stir together the tomatoes, wine, oregano, garlic, and bouillon. Pour the mixture over the chicken. Cover the slow cooker, set it to low, and let it cook for 6 to 7 hours. Add salt and pepper to taste.

YIELD: 8 servings, each with: 258 calories, 9g fat, 31g protein, 10g carbohydrate, 5g dietary fibre, 5g usable carbs.

🝑 'I've Got a Life' Chicken

This recipe from *15-Minute Low-Carb Recipes* is remarkably good. It's sweet, tangy, and fruity.

> 1.5–2kg bone-in chicken parts
> (I use legs and thighs, but a whole cut-up chicken would work great.)
> 225g sliced mushrooms
> 3 tbsps (45ml) orange juice
> Grated zest of one orange
> 1 tbsp (15ml) chicken bouillon concentrate
> 1/2 tsp pepper
> 225g tinned tomato sauce
> 2 tbsps (30ml) soy sauce
> 2 tbsps (3g) Splenda
> 1/2 tsp black treacle
> 2 tsps finely chopped garlic or 4 cloves garlic, crushed
> 1 tsp dried thyme
> Guar or xanthan

Remove the skin and any big lumps of fat from the chicken and place it in your slow cooker. (You can save time by buying chicken with the skin already removed, but it's more expensive.) Place the mushrooms on top.

In a bowl, mix together the orange juice, orange zest, bouillon, pepper, tomato sauce, soy sauce, Splenda, treacle, garlic, and thyme. Pour the mixture on top of the chicken and mushrooms. Cover the slow cooker, set it to low, and let it cook for 5 to 6 hours.

When the time's up, remove the chicken and put it on a platter. Use the guar or xanthan to thicken up the sauce in the slow cooker and serve the sauce with the chicken.

YIELD: 6 servings, each with: 424 calories, 27g fat, 35g protein, 7g carbohydrate, 1g dietary fibre, 6g usable carbs. (This analysis assumes that you eat all of the gravy.)

⛆ Slow Cooker Brewery Chicken and Vegetables

There are plenty of vegetables in here, so you don't need a thing with it, except maybe some bread for the carb-eaters in the family. And the gravy comes out a beautiful colour!

> 225g turnips (two turnips roughly the size of tennis balls),
>   peeled and cut into chunks
> 2 stalks celery, sliced
> 1 medium carrot, sliced
> 1/2 medium onion, sliced
> 1 tbsp (15ml) chicken bouillon concentrate
> 1.25–1.5kg cut-up chicken
>   (I use leg and thigh quarters, cut apart at the joints.)
> 355ml light beer
> 410g tinned tomatoes with green chiles
> Guar or xanthan (optional)

Put the turnips, celery, carrot, onion, bouillon, and chicken in your slow cooker. Pour the beer and the tomatoes over the lot. Cover the slow cooker, set it to low, and let it cook for 8 to 9 hours.

When the time's up, remove the chicken with tongs and place it on a serving platter. Then, using a slotted spoon, scoop out the vegetables. Put 350ml of them in a blender and pile the rest on and around the chicken on the platter. Scoop out about 400ml of the liquid left in the slow cooker and put it in the blender with the vegetables. Puree the veggies and stock and thicken the mixture a little more with the guar or xanthan, if it seems necessary. Add salt and pepper to taste and serve as a sauce with the chicken and vegetables.

YIELD: 5 servings, each with: 415 calories, 26g fat, 30g protein, 10g carbohydrate, 2g dietary fibre, 8g usable carbs.

Slow Cooker Chicken Guadeloupe

This isn't authentically anything, but it borrows its flavours from the Creole cooking of the Caribbean.

    1 cut-up chicken, about 1.75kg,
        or whatever chicken parts you prefer
    1/2 medium onion, chopped
    2 tsps ground allspice
    1 tsp dried thyme
    60ml lemon juice,
    410g tinned tomatoes with green chillies
    1 shot (45ml) dark rum
    Guar or xanthan

Place the chicken, onion, allspice, thyme, lemon juice, tomatoes, and rum in your slow cooker. Cover the slow cooker, set it to low, and let it cook for 5 to 6 hours.

Remove the chicken carefully – it'll be sliding from the bone! Thicken up the sauce with guar or xanthan. Add salt and pepper to taste and serve the sauce over the chicken.

YIELD: 5 servings, each with: 541 calories, 36g fat, 41g protein, 7g carbohydrate, 1g dietary fibre, 6g usable carbs.

Sort-of-Ethiopian Chicken Stew

The slow cooker method is hardly authentic, but the flavours come from an Ethiopian recipe – except that the Ethiopians would use a lot more cayenne! Increase it if you like really hot food.

1 cut-up chicken, about 1.5kg

1 medium onion, chopped

1 tsp cayenne

1 tsp paprika

1/2 tsp pepper

1/2 tsp grated ginger root

2 tbsps (30ml) lemon juice

120ml water

Guar or xanthan

Place the chicken, onion, cayenne, paprika, pepper, ginger, lemon juice, and water in your slow cooker. Cover the slow cooker, set it to low, and let it cook for 5 to 6 hours.

If you'd like to make this really stewlike, you can pick the meat off the bones when it's done (which will be very easy), thicken the gravy with guar or xanthan, and then stir the chicken back into the liquid. Or you can just serve the gravy over the chicken. Take your pick.

YIELD: 5 servings, each with: 437 calories, 31g fat, 34g protein, 3g carbohydrate, 1g dietary fibre, 2g usable carbs.

☕ Cranberry-Peach Turkey Roast

This fruity sauce really wakes up the turkey roast!

> 1.5kg turkey roast
> 2 tbsps (30ml) oil
> 50g chopped onion
> 110g cranberries
> 6g Splenda
> 3 tbsps (45g) spicy mustard
> 1/4 tsp red pepper flakes
> 1 peach, peeled and chopped

If your turkey roast is a Butterball like mine, it will be a boneless affair of light and dark meat rolled into an oval roast, enclosed in a net sack. Leave it in the net for cooking, so it doesn't fall apart.

In a big heavy skillet, heat the oil and brown the turkey on all sides. Transfer the turkey to the slow cooker.

In a blender or food processor with the S-blade in place, combine the onion, cranberries, Splenda, mustard, red pepper, and peach. Run it until you have a coarse puree. Pour the mixture over the turkey. Cover the slow cooker, set it to low, and let it cook for 6 to 7 hours.

Remove the turkey to a platter, stir up the sauce, and ladle it into a sauce boat to serve with the turkey. You can remove the net from the turkey before serving, if you like, but I find it easier just to use a good sharp knife to slice clear through the netting and let diners remove their own.

YIELD: 8 servings, each with: 255 calories, 8g fat, 31g protein, 4g carbohydrate, 1g dietary fibre, 3g usable carbs.

Braised Turkey Wings with Mushrooms

Turkey wings are my favourite cut of turkey for the slow cooker.
They fit in easily, they come in good individual serving sizes, and,
oh yeah, they taste great.

> 1.75kg turkey wings
> 60ml olive oil
> 120ml chicken stock
> 1 tsp chicken bouillon concentrate
> 1 tsp poultry seasoning
> 1 tbsp (15g) tomato paste
> 100g sliced mushrooms
> 1/2 medium onion, sliced
> 115g sour cream

In a big, heavy skillet, brown the turkey all over in the oil over medium-high heat.
Transfer the turkey to your slow cooker.

In a bowl, stir together the stock, bouillon, poultry seasoning, and tomato paste.
Pour the mixture over the turkey. Add the mushrooms and onion. Cover the slow
cooker, set it to low, and let it cook for 6 to 7 hours.

When the time's up, remove the turkey from the slow cooker with tongs. Whisk the
sour cream into the sauce and serve the sauce over the turkey.

YIELD: 3 servings, each with: 555 calories, 40g fat, 41g protein, 6g carbohydrate,
1g dietary fibre, 5g usable carbs.

Ranch-E-Que Wings

Simple!

> 1kg turkey wings
> 3 tbsps (45ml) olive oil
> 120ml chicken stock
> 3 tsps ranch-style dressing mix
> 120g Dana's 'Kansas City' Barbeque Sauce
> (see recipe page 231) or purchased low-carb barbeque sauce

Cut the turkey wings at the joints, discarding the pointy wing tips.

In a big, heavy frying pan, heat the oil and brown the turkey all over. Transfer the turkey to your slow cooker.

In a bowl, mix together the stock, dressing mix, and barbeque sauce. Pour the mixture over the wings. Cover the slow cooker, set it to low, and let it cook for 6 to 7 hours.

YIELD: 4 servings, each with: 246 calories, 17g fat, 18g protein, 5g carbohydrate, 0g dietary fibre, 5g usable carbs.

Turkey Loaf with Thai Flavours

Ground turkey is cheap, low-carb, low-calorie – and by itself just plain boring. So jazz it up by adding some Thai flavours.

> 1kg ground turkey
> 1 medium onion, chopped
> 130g tinned mushroom slices, drained
> 4 cloves garlic, crushed
> 2 tbsps (30ml) lemon juice
> 4 tbsp (60ml) lime juice, divided
> 4 tsps chilli paste
> 3 tbsps (24g) grated ginger root

1 1/2 tbsps (30g) fish sauce

1 1/2 tbsps (20ml) soy sauce

1 1/2 tsps pepper

60g pork rind crumbs

   (Run some pork scratchings through your food processor.)

10g chopped fresh coriander

120g mayonnaise

Place the turkey in a big mixing bowl.

Place the onion, mushrooms, and garlic in a food processor. Pulse until everything is chopped medium-fine. Add it to the turkey.

Add the lemon juice, 2 tbsps of the lime juice, the chilli paste, ginger, fish sauce, soy sauce, pepper, pork rind crumbs, and coriander to the bowl. Mix it around with clean hands until it is well blended.

Spray a rack or a collapsible-basket-type steamer with oil to prevent sticking and place it in your slow cooker. Add a cup of water under the rack. If the holes in the rack are pretty large, cover it with a sheet of foil, and pierce it all over with a fork. Take two 50cm squares of foil, fold them into strips about 5cm wide, and criss-cross them across the rack or steamer, running the ends up the sides of the slow cooker. (You're making a sling to help lift the meat loaf out of the slow cooker.) Place the meat mixture on the rack or steamer and form it i nto an evenly-domed loaf. Cover the slow cooker, set it to low, and let it cook for 6 hours.

When the time's up, use the strips of foil to gently lift the loaf out of the slow cooker and place it on a serving dish.

In a bowl, mix together the mayonnaise and the remaining 2 tbsps lime juice. Cut the loaf into wedges and serve it with the lime mayonnaise.

YIELD: 8 servings, each with: 327 calories, 24g fat, 25g protein, 5g carbohydrate, 1g dietary fibre, 4g usable carbs.

Chipotle Turkey Legs

This dish has spicy, rich Southwestern flavour.

    3 turkey drumsticks, about 1kg total

    1 1/2 tsps cumin

    1 tsp chilli powder

    1 tsp dried, powdered sage

    1 tsp finely chopped garlic or 2 cloves garlic, crushed

    1/2 tsp red pepper flakes

    1/4 tsp turmeric

    1 or 2 tinned chipotle chiles in adobo sauce, plus a couple tsps
       of the sauce they come in (found in delis and gourmet food shops, and
       online, try www.coolchile.co.uk)

    225g tomato sauce

    1 tbsp (15g) Worcestershire sauce

    Guar or xanthan

    6 tbsps (60g) grated queso quesadilla* or semi-soft, smoked cheese (optional)

Place the turkey in your slow cooker. (If you can fit more, feel free. My 3-litre slow cooker will only hold 3.)

In a blender, combine the cumin, chilli powder, sage, garlic, red pepper flakes, turmeric, chillies, tomato sauce, and Worcestershire sauce. Run it for a minute, then pour the mixture over the turkey. Cover the slow cooker, set it to low, and let it cook for 5 to 6 hours.

When the time's up, remove each turkey leg to a serving plate, thicken the sauce with guar or xanthan, and spoon the sauce over the turkey legs. If you like, sprinkle 2 tbsps of grated cheese over each turkey leg and let it melt for a minute or two before serving.

* This is a mild, white Mexican cheese.

YIELD: 3 servings, each with: 451 calories, 22g fat, 54g protein, 9g carbohydrate, 2g dietary fibre, 7g usable carbs. (Analysis depends on the size of the turkey leg.)

Turkey with Mushroom Sauce

1.5kg boneless, skinless turkey breast (in one big hunk, not thin cutlets)

30g butter

16g chopped fresh parsley

2 tsps dried tarragon

1/2 tsp salt or Vege-Sal

1/4 tsp pepper

100g sliced mushrooms

120ml dry white wine

1 tsp chicken bouillon concentrate

Guar or xanthan (optional)

In a big, heavy frying pan, sauté the turkey in the butter until it's golden all over. Transfer the turkey to your slow cooker.

Sprinkle the parsley, tarragon, salt or Vege-Sal, and pepper over the turkey. Place the mushrooms on top.

In a bowl, mix the wine and bouillon together until the bouillon dissolves. Pour it over the turkey. Cover the slow cooker, set it to low, and let it cook for 7 to 8 hours.

When the time's up, remove the turkey and put it on a serving dish. Transfer about half of the mushrooms to a blender and add the liquid from the slow cooker. Blend until the mushrooms are pureed. Scoop the rest of the mushrooms into the dish you plan to use to serve the sauce, add the liquid, and thicken further with guar or xanthan, if needed.

YIELD: 8 servings, each with: 281 calories, 14g fat, 34g protein, 1g carbohydrate, trace dietary fibre, 1g usable carbs.

CHAPTER FOUR

Slow Cooker Beef

Tired of steaks and burgers? Use your slow cooker, and you'll be on your way to beef stews, pot roasts, chilli, and other classic comfort foods – all waiting when you get home!

🍲 New England Boiled Dinner

This is our traditional St. Patrick's Day dinner, but it's a simple, satisfying one-pot meal on any chilly night. This is easy, but it takes a long time to cook. Do yourself a favour, and assemble it ahead of time. If you have carb-eaters in the family, you can add a few little red potatoes, still in their jackets, to this.

6 small turnips, peeled and quartered

2 large stalks celery, cut into chunks

2 medium onions, cut into chunks

1.5kg corned beef

1/2 head cabbage, cut into wedges

Spicy brown mustard

Horseradish

Butter

Place the turnips in your slow cooker, along with the celery and the onions. Set the corned beef on top and add water to cover. There will be a seasoning packet with the corned beef, empty it into the slow cooker. Cover the slow cooker, set it to low, and let it cook for 10 to 12 hours. (You can cut the cooking time down to 6 to 8 hours if you set the slow cooker to high, but the low setting yields the most tender results.)

When the time's up, remove the corned beef from the slow cooker with a fork or tongs, put the lid back on the slow cooker to retain heat, put the beef on a serving dish, and keep it someplace warm. Place the cabbage in the slow cooker with the other vegetables. Re-cover the slow cooker, set it to high, and let it cook for 1/2 hour.

With a slotted spoon, remove all the vegetables and pile them around the corned beef on the serving dish. Serve with the mustard and horseradish as condiments for the beef and butter for the vegetables.

YIELD: 8 servings, each with: 372 calories, 25g fat, 26g protein, 9g carbohydrate, 2g dietary fibre, 7g usable carbs.

⊙ Maple-Glazed Corned Beef with Vegetables

This is a trifle less traditional than, but just as good as, the New England Boiled Dinner (see recipe on previous page). The pancake syrup and mustard, plus last-minute glazing under the grill, give it a new aspect.

> 6 medium turnips, cut into chunks
> 2 medium carrots, cut into chunks
> 1 medium onion, quartered
> 2.5kg corned beef brisket
> 470ml water
> 1 medium head cabbage, cut into wedges
> 3 tbsps (30g) sugar-free pancake syrup
> 1 tbsp (15g) brown mustard
> Horseradish

Place the turnips, carrots, and onion in your slow cooker. Place the corned beef on top. Scatter the contents of the accompanying seasoning packet over everything and pour the water over the whole thing. Cover the slow cooker, set it to low, and let it cook for 9 to 10 hours, and a bit more won't hurt!

When the time's up, carefully remove the corned beef and put it on your grill rack, fatty side up. Use a slotted spoon to skim out the vegetables, put them on a serving dish, cover, and keep in a warm place.

Place the cabbage in the slow cooker, set it to high, and let it cook for 15 to 20 minutes, or until just tender. (Or you can pour the liquid from the pot into a saucepan and cook the cabbage in it on your stovetop, which is faster.)

While the cabbage is cooking, mix together the pancake syrup and the mustard. Spread the mixture over the corned beef, just the side that is up. When the cabbage is almost done, run the corned beef under your grill for 2 to 3 minutes, until glazed.

Transfer the cabbage to the serving dish with a slotted spoon. Slice the corned beef across the grain and serve immediately.

Serve this with horseradish and mustard.

YIELD: 12 servings, each with: 416 calories, 28g fat, 29g protein, 10g carbohydrate, 3g dietary fibre, 7g usable carbs. (This carb count does not include the polyols in the pancake syrup.)

⛪ Asian Slow Cooker Small Ribs

Look for black bean sauce in Asian markets or in the international aisle of a big supermarket. You'll only use a little at a time, but it keeps a long time in the fridge, and it adds authenticity to Asian dishes.

3kg beef small ribs
3 tbsps (45ml) oil
1 stalk celery, chopped
30g grated carrot
50g chopped onion
2 tbsps (16g) grated ginger root
6 tsps Chinese black bean sauce
3 tsps chilli garlic paste
3 cloves garlic, crushed
60ml soy sauce
235ml dry red wine
475ml beef stock
1 tsp five-spice powder
1 tbsp (1.5g) Splenda
Guar or xanthan

In a big, heavy frying pan, brown the ribs all over in the oil. Transfer the ribs to your slow cooker.

Add the celery, carrot, and onion to the frying pan and sauté over medium-high heat until they soften and start to brown. Stir in the ginger, black bean sauce, chilli garlic paste, and garlic and sauté for another couple of minutes. Now stir in the soy sauce, wine, stock, five-spice powder, and Splenda. Pour the mixture over the ribs. Cover the slow cooker, set it to low, and let it cook for 6 to 7 hours.

When the time's up, transfer the ribs to a serving dish and scoop the vegetables into a blender with a slotted spoon. Add 2 cups of the liquid and run the blender till the vegetables are pureed. Thicken the sauce to a double cream consistency with guar or xanthan and serve the sauce with the ribs.

YIELD: 12 servings, each with: 948 calories, 86g fat, 35g protein, 3g carbohydrate, trace dietary fibre, 3g usable carbs.

⌒ Balsamic Pot Roast

Balsamic vinegar and rosemary give this pot roast an Italian accent.

1.75kg beef round, trimmed of fat

2 tbsps (30ml) olive oil

1 large onion, sliced

2 cloves garlic, crushed

235ml beef stock

1 tsp beef bouillon concentrate

60ml balsamic vinegar

$1/2$ tsp dried rosemary, ground

260g tinned chopped tomatoes

Guar or xanthan

In a big, heavy frying pan, sear the beef in the oil until browned all over. Transfer the beef to your slow cooker. Scatter the onion and garlic around the beef.

In a bowl, stir together the stock, bouillon, vinegar, and rosemary. Pour the mixture over the beef. Pour the tomatoes on top. Season with pepper. Cover the slow cooker, set it to low, and let it cook for 8 hours.

When the time's up, remove the beef with tongs and place it on a serving plate. Scoop the onions out with a slotted spoon and pile them around the roast. Thicken the juice left in the slow cooker with guar or xanthan and serve it with the beef.

YIELD: 8 servings, each with: 451 calories, 29g fat, 42g protein, 5g carbohydrate, trace dietary fibre, 5g usable carbs.

Bavarian Pot Roast

Given the Bavarian theme, I reckon Fauxtatoes (see recipe page 239) and cooked cabbage are the obvious side dishes with this.

1 large red onion, sliced 3cm thick

2 tbsps (3g) Splenda

1/4 tsp black treacle

2 tbsps (30ml) cider vinegar

1 tsp salt

1 tsp beef bouillon concentrate

1.25kg beef round, trimmed of fat and cubed

Guar or xanthan (optional)

Place the onion in your slow cooker.

In a bowl, mix together the Splenda, treacle, vinegar, salt, and bouillon. Pour the mixture over the onion. Place the beef on top. Cover the slow cooker, set it to low, and let it cook for 7 to 8 hours.

When the time's up, thicken the stock with guar or xanthan if desired.

YIELD: 8 servings, each with: 297 calories, 18g fat, 29g protein, 2g carbohydrate, trace dietary fibre, 2g usable carbs.

Beef and Broccoli

This doesn't come out exactly like stir-fry, but it's still Chinese-y-good, and it's a lot less last-minute trouble.

  450g lean beef, cut into 3cm cubes
  120g tinned, sliced mushrooms, drained
  1 medium onion, cut into wedges
  120ml beef stock
  1 tsp beef bouillon concentrate
  1 tbsp (1.5g) Splenda
  1 tsp grated ginger root
  1 tbsp (15ml) dry sherry
  2 tbsps (28ml soy sauce
  1 clove garlic, crushed
  1 tsp dark sesame oil
  1 tbsp (7g) sesame seeds
  500g frozen broccoli florets
  Guar or xanthan

Combine the beef, mushrooms, onion, stock, bouillon, Splenda, ginger, sherry, soy sauce, garlic, and sesame oil in your slow cooker. Sprinkle the sesame seeds on top. Cover the slow cooker, set it to low, and let it cook for 8 to 10 hours.

When the time's up, add the broccoli to the slow cooker, re-cover the slow cooker, and let it cook for another 30 minutes. Thicken the juices a little with guar or xanthan.

Serve over Cauli-Rice (see recipe page 239) if desired.

YIELD: 4 servings, each with: 314 calories, 17g fat, 29g protein, 10g carbohydrate, 4g dietary fibre, 6g usable carbs.

⚏ Beef Carbonnade

Très French!

    1kg lean beef, cut into 3cm cubes

    2 tbsps (30ml) olive oil

    1 large onion, sliced

    2 medium carrots, cut 3cm thick

    2 turnips, cubed

    350ml light beer

    60ml red wine vinegar

    3 tbsps (4.5g) Splenda

    1/4 tsp black treacle

    235ml beef stock

    2 tsps beef bouillon concentrate

    3 cloves garlic, crushed

    2 tsps dried thyme

    2 tsps Worcestershire sauce

    1/2 tsp pepper

    2 bay leaves

    Guar or xanthan

In a big, heavy frying pan, sear the beef all over in the oil. Place the beef in your slow cooker. Add the onion, carrots, and turnips and stir everything around a bit.

In a bowl, mix together the beer, vinegar, Splenda, treacle, stock, bouillon, garlic, thyme, Worcestershire sauce, and pepper. Pour the mixture into the slow cooker. Throw the bay leaves on top. Cover the slow cooker, set it to low, and let it cook for 8 hours.

When the time's up, remove the bay leaves and add guar or xanthan to thicken the sauce a bit.

You can serve this as is, or, to be more traditional, serve it over Fauxtatoes (see recipe page 239).

YIELD: 6 servings, each with: 411 calories, 24g fat, 34g protein, 10g carbohydrate, 2g dietary fibre, 8g usable carbs.

⊙ Sauerbrauten

This classic German pot roast takes advance planning, but it's not a lot of work, and it gives impressive results. Don't forget the Fauxtatoes (see recipe page 239) for that gravy!

2kg boneless lean beef
235ml cider vinegar
1 cup water
1/2 onion, sliced
2 bay leaves
1 tsp pepper
6g Splenda
2 tbsps (30ml) bacon grease or oil
1/4 tsp ground ginger
240g light sour cream
(Use full-fat sour cream if you prefer, but it's no lower carb.)
Guar or xanthan (optional)

Pierce the beef all over with a fork. In a deep, non-reactive bowl (stainless steel, glass, or enamel), combine the vinegar, water, onion, bay leaves, pepper, and Splenda. Place the beef in the marinade and put the bowl in the refrigerator. Marinate the beef for at least 3 days, and 5 or 6 days won't hurt. Turn it over at least once a day, so both sides marinate evenly.

When the time comes to cook your Sauerbrauten, remove the beef from the marinade and pat it dry with paper towels. Reserve the marinade.

In a big, heavy frying pan, heat the bacon grease or oil and sear the beef all over. Transfer the beef to your slow cooker.

Scoop the onion and bay leaves out of the marinade with a slotted spoon and put them on top of the beef. Remove 250ml of the marinade from the bowl and add the ginger to it. Pour this over the beef and discard the remaining marinade. Cover the slow cooker, set it to low, and let it cook for 7 to 8 hours.

When the time's up, remove the beef to a serving plate. Stir the sour cream into the liquid in the slow cooker and thicken it if you think it needs it with guar or xanthan. Add salt and pepper to taste and serve the sauce with the beef.

YIELD: 10 servings, each with: 407 calories, 26g fat, 38g protein, 3g carbohydrate, trace dietary fibre, 3g usable carbs.

Beef Stroganoff

This creamy gravy is fabulous!

    1kg lean beef, cut into 3cm cubes

    1 large onion, chopped

    225g tinned, sliced mushrooms, undrained

    425ml tinned beef stock

    1 tsp beef bouillon concentrate

    2 tsps Worcestershire sauce

    1 tsp paprika

    225g cream cheese (regular or light)

    225g sour cream (regular or light)

Put the beef in your slow cooker. Put the onion on top, then dump in the mushrooms, liquid and all.

In a bowl, mix the beef stock with the bouillon, Worcestershire sauce, and paprika. Pour the mixture into the slow cooker. Cover the slow cooker, set it to low, and let it cook for 8 to 10 hours.

When the time's up, cut the cream cheese into cubes and stir it into the mixture in the slow cooker until melted. Stir in the sour cream.

Serve over Fauxtatoes (see recipe page 239) or Cauli-Rice (see recipe page 239), if desired. Actually, because noodles are traditional with Stroganoff this would be a good place to serve low-carb pasta, if you have a brand you like.

> **NOTE:** This can be made with plain yogurt in place of both the cream cheese and sour cream. After getting everything together in the slow cooker and starting the cooking, place a strainer in a bowl. Line the strainer with a clean coffee filter and pour two 230ml containers of plain yogurt into it. Set the strainer and bowl in the refrigerator and let the yogurt drain all day. Whisk the resulting yogurt cheese into your Stroganoff in place of cream cheese and sour cream.

YIELD: 8 servings, each with: 413 calories, 31g fat, 28g protein, 5g carbohydrate, 1g dietary fibre, 4g usable carbs.

Beef with Asian Mushroom Sauce

Once you have the Hoisin Sauce on hand, this is very quick to put together. The Hoisin Sauce is really easy, and it keeps well in the fridge.

    115g sliced mushrooms
    2kg beef tip roast
    60ml Hoisin Sauce (see recipe page 233)
    2 cloves garlic, finely chopped
    1/2 tsp salt
    60ml beef stock
    Guar or xanthan
    35g sliced spring onions

Put the mushrooms in your slow cooker and place the beef on top. Spread the Hoisin Sauce over the beef, scatter the garlic and salt over it, and pour in the stock around it. Cover the slow cooker, set it to low, and let it cook for 9 hours.

When the time's up, remove the beef from the slow cooker and put it on a serving dish.

Add guar or xanthan to thicken up the sauce a bit and then pour the sauce into a sauce boat. Slice the beef and serve it with the sauce, topped with the spring onions.

YIELD: 6 servings, each with: 658 calories, 43g fat, 61g protein, 4g carbohydrate, 1g dietary fibre, 3g usable carbs.

⊡ Small Ribs with Wine and Mushrooms

Small ribs are very flavourful, and this is a simple way to make the most of them.

    2kg beef small ribs
    2 bay leaves
    1 tbsp (15g) Worcestershire sauce
    1 tbsp (15ml) beef bouillon concentrate
    120ml dry red wine
    225g tinned mushrooms, drained
    Guar or xanthan

Place the ribs in your slow cooker. Add the bay leaves, Worcestershire sauce, and bouillon. Pour the wine over everything. Place the mushrooms on top. Cover the slow cooker, set it to low, and let it cook for 8 to 10 hours.

When the time's up, use a slotted spoon to scoop out the ribs and mushrooms and put them on a serving dish. There may be a fair amount of grease on the liquid in the pot; it's best to skim it off. Thicken the sauce to taste with guar or xanthan.

Fauxtatoes (see recipe page 239) are the ideal side with this, so you have something to eat all that gravy on!

YIELD: 10 servings, each with: 388 calories, 22g fat, 42g protein, 1g carbohydrate, trace dietary fibre, 1g usable carbs.

Small Rib Stew

1.5kg small beef ribs

2 tbsps (30ml) olive oil

1 medium onion, chopped

225g sliced mushrooms

350ml beef stock

$1/2$ tsp pepper

$1/2$ tsp dried marjoram

$1/2$ tsp caraway seeds

1 tbsp (15ml) lemon juice

2 tbsps (30ml) red wine vinegar

1 tsp beef bouillon concentrate

In a big, heavy frying pan, brown the ribs all over in the oil over medium-high heat. Transfer the ribs to your slow cooker. In the frying pan, over medium-low heat, sauté the onion and mushrooms until they're just softened. Transfer them to the slow cooker, too.

In a bowl, mix together the stock, pepper, marjoram, caraway seeds, lemon juice, vinegar, and bouillon. Pour the mixture over the ribs. Cover the slow cooker, set it to low, and let it cook for 7 to 8 hours.

You can thicken the pot liquid if you like, but I rather like this as is, especially with Fauxtatoes (see recipe page 239).

YIELD: 6 servings, each with: 955 calories, 87g fat, 36g protein, 5g carbohydrate, 1g dietary fibre, 4g usable carbs.

Stewing Steak with Avocado Aioli

This was a big hit with our tester's family!

1.5kg boneless stewing steak

1 tbsp (15ml) olive oil

1 medium onion, finely chopped

120ml water

1 tsp beef bouillon concentrate

50g Worcestershire sauce

1 tsp dried oregano

1 clove garlic, crushed

Avocado Aioli (see recipe on next page)

Season the beef with salt and pepper.

In a big, heavy frying pan, sear the beef all over in the oil. Transfer the beef to your slow cooker. Add the onion.

In a bowl, combine the water and bouillon. Pour it over the beef. Add the Worcestershire sauce, oregano, and garlic. Cover the slow cooker, set it to low, and let it cook for 8 hours.

Serve with the Avocado Aioli.

YIELD: 8 servings, each with: 381 calories, 28g fat, 27g protein, 3g carbohydrate, trace dietary fibre, 3g usable carbs.

🫙 Avocado Aioli

You don't have to reserve this for use with the Stewing Steak with Avocado Aioli (see recipe on previous page). Serve it as a dip with vegetables, too. California avocados are the little, black, rough-skinned ones, and they're lower in carbs than the big, green, smooth-skinned Florida avocados.

2 ripe California avocados
60g mayonnaise
1 tbsp (15ml) lime juice
1–2 cloves garlic, crushed
1/4 tsp salt

Scoop the avocado flesh into a blender or food processor. Add the mayonnaise, lime juice, garlic, and salt and process until smooth.

YIELD: 8 servings, each with: 127 calories, 13g fat, 1g protein, 3g carbohydrate, 2g dietary fibre, 1g usable carbs.

⊡ Steak Chunks in Gravy

This is a great home-cooked dish will stick to your ribs.

   1 tbsp (15ml) olive oil
   700g steak cut into 4cm chunks
   1 medium onion, sliced
   225g sliced mushrooms
   700ml beef stock
   1 tbsp (15ml) beef bouillon concentrate
   Guar or xanthan

In a big, heavy frying pan, heat the oil and brown the steaks on both sides.

Put the onion and mushrooms in your slow cooker.

In a bowl, stir the stock and bouillon and pour the mixture over the veggies. Place the steaks on top. Cover the slow cooker, set it to low, and let it cook for 6 to 7 hours.

When the time's up, remove the steaks and thicken the sauce with guar or xanthan to your liking.

Serve with Fauxtatoes (see recipe page 239).

YIELD: 6 servings, each with: 297 calories, 17g fat, 29g protein, 5g carbohydrate, 1g dietary fibre, 4g usable carbs.

⌐ Easy Italian Beef

This is just so easy but full of flavour!

> 2 tbsps (30ml) olive oil
> 1kg beef stewing steak, trimmed of fat
> 120ml beef stock
> 1 tbsp (15ml) beef bouillon concentrate
> 1 pack (20g) Italian salad dressing mix

In a big, heavy frying pan, heat the oil over medium-high heat and brown the beef on both sides. Transfer the beef to your slow cooker.

In a bowl, combine the stock, bouillon, and salad dressing mix. Pour the mixture over the beef. Cover the slow cooker, set it to low, and let it cook for 6 to 8 hours.

YIELD: 4 servings, each with: 543 calories, 42g fat, 37g protein, 1g carbohydrate, 0g dietary fibre, 1g usable carbs.

Roman Stew

Instead of using the usual Italian seasonings, this was adapted from a historic Roman stew recipe, using spices from the Far East. It's unusual and wonderful.

  1.5kg beef stewing steak, cut into 3cm cubes

  3 tbsps (45ml) olive oil

  4 cloves garlic

  240g sliced celery

  1 tsp salt or Vege-Sal

  1/4 tsp ground cinnamon

  1/4 tsp ground cloves

  1/4 tsp pepper

  1/8 tsp ground allspice

  1/8 tsp ground nutmeg

  410g tinned diced tomatoes, undrained

  120ml dry red wine

  Guar or xanthan (optional)

In a big, heavy frying pan, brown the beef in the oil over medium-high heat, in a few batches. Transfer the beef to your slow cooker. Add the garlic and celery to the slow cooker, then sprinkle the salt or Vege-Sal, cinnamon, cloves, pepper, allspice, and nutmeg over the beef and vegetables. Pour the tomatoes and the wine over the beef and vegetables. Cover the slow cooker, set it to low, and let it cook for 7 to 8 hours.

You can thicken the pot juices a little if you like with guar or xanthan, but it's not really necessary.

YIELD: 8 servings, each with: 369 calories, 17g fat, 44g protein, 5g carbohydrate, 1g dietary fibre, 4g usable carbs.

Mexican Stew

This Tex-Mex dinner is a simple family-pleaser.

> 1kg beef stew meat, cut into 3cm cubes
> 410g tinned tomatoes with green chiles
> 50g sliced onion
> 1 tsp chilli powder
> 1 envelope (35g) taco seasoning mix
>   (sometimes sold as mexican seasoning)
> 425g tinned black soybeans
> 115g sour cream

Put the beef, tomatoes, onion, and chilli powder in your slow cooker. Cover the slow cooker, set it to low, and let it cook for 8 to 9 hours.

Stir in the taco seasoning and soybeans. Re-cover the slow cooker, turn it to high, and let it cook for another 20 minutes. Place a dollop of sour cream on each serving.

This makes 6 generous servings, and it could even serve 8.

YIELD: 6 servings, each with: 399 calories, 18g fat, 46g protein, 12g carbohydrate, 5g dietary fibre, 7g usable carbs.

⊙ Comfort Food Casserole

This is one of those meal-in-a-bowl type of things that just seem – well, comforting, somehow. I've found that slow cooking really brings out the best in turnips. They end up remarkably like potatoes.

> 700g lean beef mince
> 1 tbsp (14ml) oil
> 1 medium onion, chopped
> 4 cloves garlic, crushed
> 4 stalks celery, diced
> 235ml beef stock
> 1 tsp beef bouillon concentrate
> 1/2 tsp salt or Vege-Sal
> 1 tsp pepper
> 2 tsps dried oregano
> 1 tsp dry mustard
> 2 tbsps (32g) tomato paste
> 115g cream cheese
> 3 turnips, cubed
> 80g grated cheddar cheese

In a big, heavy frying pan, brown and crumble the beef over medium-high heat. Pour off the fat and transfer the beef to your slow cooker.

Add the oil to the frying pan and reduce the heat to medium-low. Add the onion, garlic, and celery and sauté until they're just softened. Add the stock, bouillon, salt or Vege-Sal, pepper, oregano, dry mustard, and tomato paste and stir. Now add the cream cheese, using the edge of a spatula to cut the cream cheese into chunks. Let this mixture simmer, stirring occasionally, until the cream cheese is melted.

Meanwhile add the turnips to the slow cooker.

When the cream cheese has melted into the sauce, pour the sauce into the slow cooker. Stir until the ground beef and turnips are coated. Cover the slow cooker, set it to low, and let it cook for 6 hours. Serve with cheddar cheese on top.

YIELD: 6 servings, each with: 549 calories, 40g fat, 35g protein, 12g carbohydrate, 3g dietary fibre, 9g usable carbs.

Firehouse Chilli

Here's a crowd-pleaser! I served this on a rainy afternoon at our local campground and made a lot of friends! You could halve this, but you'd be left with a half a tin of soybeans, and you know you'll eat it up, so why bother?

1kg lean beef mince

150g chopped onion

4 cloves garlic, crushed

3 tbsps (20g) chilli powder

3 tsps paprika

4 tsps ground cumin

60g Dana's No-Sugar Ketchup (see recipe page 228)
    or purchased low-carb ketchup

2 tbsps (30g) tomato paste

410g tinned diced tomatoes

350ml light beer

1 tsp Splenda

2 1/2 tsps salt

425g tinned black soybeans

In a big, heavy frying pan, brown and crumble the beef over medium-high heat. Drain it and place it in your slow cooker. Add the onion, garlic, chilli powder, paprika, cumin, ketchup, tomato paste, tomatoes, beer, Splenda, salt, and soybeans. Stir everything up. Cover the slow cooker, set it to low, and let it cook for 8 hours.

This is good with grated cheese and sour cream. What chilli isn't? But it also stands on its own very well.

YIELD: 10 servings, each with: 329 calories, 21g fat, 21g protein, 12g carbohydrate, 4g dietary fibre, 8g usable carbs.

Carne all'Ungherese

The original recipe, from which I adapted this, said it was an Italian version of a Hungarian stew. Whatever it is, it's good!

60ml olive oil
700g stewing steak, cut into 3cm cubes
1 medium onion, chopped
1 green pepper, cut into strips
2 cloves garlic, crushed
235ml beef stock
1 tsp beef bouillon concentrate
1 tsp dried marjoram
1 tbsp (16g) tomato paste
1 tbsp (7g) paprika
1 tbsp (30ml) lemon juice
125g plain yogurt

In a big, heavy frying pan, heat a tbsp or two of the oil over medium-high heat. Start browning the stew meat. It will take two or three batches; add more oil as you need it. Transfer each batch of browned meat to your slow cooker as it's done.

When all the meat is browned, put the last of the oil in the frying pan, reduce the heat to medium-low, and add the onion. Sauté the onion until it's just softening and add it to the slow cooker. Add the green pepper to the slow cooker.

In a bowl, mix together the garlic, stock, bouillon, marjoram, tomato paste, paprika, and lemon juice, stirring until the bouillon and tomato paste are dissolved. Pour the mixture over the meat and onions. Cover the slow cooker, set it to low, and let it cook for 6 to 7 hours.

When the time's up, stir in the yogurt.

Serve over Fauxtatoes (see recipe page 239).

YIELD: 5 servings, each with: 382 calories, 22g fat, 38g protein, 7g carbohydrate, 1g dietary fibre, 6g usable carbs. (Analysis does not include Fauxtatoes.)

Swiss Steak

Here's a no-work version of this old-time favourite.

1 large onion, sliced

1.5kg stewing steak

1 tbsp (15ml) beef bouillon concentrate

235ml vegetable juice (such as V8)

2 stalks celery, sliced

Guar or xanthan (optional)

Place the onion in your slow cooker. Place the beef on top.

In a bowl, stir the bouillon into the vegetable juice. Pour the mixture over the beef. Scatter the celery on top. Cover the slow cooker, set it to low, and let it cook for 8 to 10 hours.

When the time's up, thicken the juices with guar or xanthan if desired.

Serve over pureed cauliflower.

YIELD: 8 servings, each with: 360 calories, 22g fat, 35g protein, 3g carbohydrate, 1g dietary fibre, 2g usable carbs.

Beef and Courgette Stew

Don't try adding the courgettes at the beginning, or they'll cook to a mush! Put out some vegetables and dip for the ravening hoards, and sip a glass of wine while you're waiting that last hour.

1kg boneless beef stewing steak, trimmed of fat

1 medium onion, sliced

1 large red bell pepper, cut into 3cm squares

1 large green bell pepper, cut into 3cm squares

250g no-sugar-added spaghetti sauce

120ml beef stock

1/2 tsp beef bouillon concentrate

700g courgette, cut into 2cm slices

Guar or xanthan (optional)

In your slow cooker, combine the beef with the onion and peppers.

In a bowl, stir together the spaghetti sauce, stock, and bouillon. Pour the mixture over the beef and vegetables and stir. Cover the slow cooker, set it to low, and let it cook for 9 hours.

Turn the slow cooker to high, stir in the courgette, re-cover, and let it cook for 1 more hour.

When the time's up, thicken the sauce with guar or xanthan if needed.

YIELD: 6 servings, each with: 367 calories, 24g fat, 27g protein, 10g carbohydrate, 3g dietary fibre, 7g usable carbs.

Chipotle Brisket

Our tester, who loved this recipe, halved it. You can feel free to do the same.

> 2kg beef brisket, cut into pieces if necessary
>   to fit into your slow cooker
> 2 tbsps (30ml) olive oil
> 1 medium onion, thinly sliced
> 4 stalks celery, thinly sliced
> 4 cloves garlic, crushed
> 1 tbsp (10g) dry mustard
> 1 tbsp (4g) dried oregano
> 1 tsp ground cumin
> 2 tsps pepper
> 1 tsp salt or Vege-Sal
> 450g tinned tomato sauce
> 1/2 cup (120ml beef stock
> 1 tsp beef bouillon concentrate
> 60ml red wine vinegar
> 12g Splenda
> 1/2 tsp black treacle
> 2 chipotle chiles tinned in adobo sauce
> 2 bay leaves
> Guar or xanthan

In a big, heavy frying pan, brown the beef all over in the oil over medium-high heat. Transfer the beef to your slow cooker.

Add the onion and celery to the frying pan and sauté until softened. Stir in the garlic, dry mustard, oregano, cumin, pepper, and salt or Vege-Sal and sauté for another minute or two. Transfer the mixture to the slow cooker, on top of the brisket.

In a blender or food processor, combine the tomato sauce, stock, bouillon, vinegar, Splenda, treacle, and chipotles and blend until smooth.

Put the bay leaves in the slow cooker, on top of the beef, and pour the sauce over the whole thing. Cover the slow cooker, set it to low, and let it cook for 12 hours.

When the time's up, remove the beef to a serving dish. Thicken the sauce to taste with guar or xanthan and serve the sauce over the beef.

YIELD: 8 servings, each with: 779 calories, 64g fat, 41g protein, 8g carbohydrate, 2g dietary fibre, 6g usable carbs.

Simple Salsa Beef

Here's one of those extra-simple chuck-it-in-and-go recipes. It's great for a day when you didn't get dinner in the slow cooker the night before!

3 turnips, peeled and cubed
450g baby carrots
1.5kg beef pot roast
520g salsa
Guar or xanthan (optional)

Put the turnips and carrots in your slow cooker, then place the beef on top. Pour the salsa over the lot. Cover the slow cooker, set it to low, and let it cook for 8 to 10 hours.

When the time's up, remove the beef and pull it apart into shreds with two forks. Scoop the vegetables out onto serving plates with a slotted spoon. Pile the beef on top. If desired, thicken the sauce with a little guar or xanthan. Spoon the sauce over the vegetables and beef.

YIELD: 8 servings, each with: 200 calories, 5g fat, 26g protein, 11g carbohydrate, 3g dietary fibre, 8g usable carbs.

Oxtails Pontchartrain

This has a lot of American South, New Orleans elements, including some serious heat, so I named it after Lake Pontchartrain. Oxtails are bony, but very flavourful, and they take very well to the slow cooker. If you haven't had oxtails, don't fear them; they're just muscle meat, like a steak or a roast. It's just that there's a high bone-to-meat ratio.

2kg beef oxtails
3 tbsps (18g) Cajun seasoning
2 tbsps (30ml) olive oil
3 large banana peppers, sliced
1 medium onion, sliced
1 medium carrot, grated
2 stalks celery, sliced
1 clove garlic, crushed
235ml dry red wine
60ml brandy
1 1/2 tsps dried thyme
3 bay leaves
410g tinned diced tomatoes
2 chipotle chiles tinned in adobo sauce, chopped
(You can use just one if you'd like to cut the heat a bit.)

Sprinkle the oxtails all over with the Cajun seasoning.

In a big, heavy frying pan, heat the oil and brown the oxtails all over. Transfer the oxtails to your slow cooker.

Add the peppers, onion, carrot, celery, and garlic to the frying pan and sauté them until they're just softened. Add them to the slow cooker, too, and mix them in with the oxtails.

Pour the wine and brandy in the frying pan and stir it around. Stir in the thyme and add the bay leaves, tomatoes, and chipotles. Stir this all up and pour it over the oxtails and veggies. Cover the slow cooker, set it to low, and let it cook for 8 hours.

YIELD: 6 servings each with: 935 calories, 48g fat, 96g protein, 13g carbohydrate, 3g dietary fibre, 10g usable carbs.

3-Minute Slow Cooker Pot Roast

This recipe, originally from *15-Minute Low-Carb Recipes*, is very 1965, but it's still incredibly easy, and it tastes great.

> 225g sliced mushrooms
> 1–1.5kg boneless stewing steak
> 1 envelope (23g) French onion soup mix
> 120ml dry red wine
> Guar or xanthan

Place the mushrooms in the bottom of your slow cooker and add the beef on top of them.

In a bowl, mix together the onion soup mix and wine and pour it into the slow cooker. Cover the slow cooker, set it to low, and let it cook for 8 hours.

When the time's up, remove the beef (carefully – it will be very tender) and use the guar or xanthan to thicken the juices in the slow cooker. Serve this gravy with the pot roast.

YIELD: 6 servings, each with: 358 calories, 24g fat, 25g protein, 6g carbohydrate, 1g dietary fibre, 5g usable carbs. (This analysis assumes you use a 2-pound roast and that you eat every drop of the gravy.)

⊡ Pepperoncini Beef

Pepperoncini are hot-but-not-scorching pickled Italian salad peppers. You'll find these in the same aisle as the olives and pickles. They make this beef very special. If you can't find pepperoncini, try pickled cherry peppers.

> 1–1.5kg boneless stewing steak
> 120g pepperoncini peppers, undrained
> 1/2 medium onion, chopped
> Guar or xanthan

Place the beef in your slow cooker, pour the peppers on top, and strew the onion over that. Cover the slow cooker, set it to low, and let it cook for 8 hours.

When the time's up, remove the beef, put it on a serving dish, and use a slotted spoon to scoop out the peppers and pile them on top of the beef. Thicken the juices in the pot with the guar or xanthan. Add salt and pepper to taste and serve the sauce with the beef.

YIELD: 6 servings, each with: 325 calories, 24g fat, 24g protein, 3g carbohydrate, trace dietary fibre, 3g usable carbs. (This analysis is for a 2-pound roast.)

⌂ Beef in Beer

Here's a simple recipe from *500 Low-Carb Recipes*. The tea, the beer, and the long, slow cooking make this as tender as can be. I've changed this just a little. Originally, you dredged the beef in soy powder or low-carb bake mix, but I've decided that's inessential. And it's another step, and a messy one at that.

> 2-3 tbsps (30-45ml) olive oil
>
> 1kg boneless stewing steak
>
> 1 medium onion, sliced
>
> 225g tinned tomato sauce
>
> 350ml light beer
>
> 1 tsp instant tea powder (try the Whittard's brand)
>
> 115g tinned mushrooms, drained
>
> 2 cloves garlic, crushed

Heat oil in a big, heavy frying pan over medium-high heat and sear the beef until it's brown all over. Transfer the beef to your slow cooker.

In the oil left in the frying pan, fry the onion for a few minutes and add that to the slow cooker, too.

Pour the tomato sauce and beer over the beef. Sprinkle the tea over it and add the mushrooms and garlic. Cover the slow cooker, set it to low, and let it cook for 8 to 9 hours.

This is good served with Fauxtatoes (recipe page 239).

YIELD: 6 servings, each with: 374 calories, 24g fat, 28g protein, 7g carbohydrate, 2g dietary fibre, 5g usable carbs.

🍲 Peking Slow Cooker Pot Roast

This sounds nuts, but it tastes great! This recipe, originally from
500 Low-Carb Recipes, means starting ahead, but it's not a lot of work.

    1.5–2.5kg beef (stewing or other inexpensive cuts)
    5 or 6 cloves garlic, sliced thin
    235ml cider vinegar
    235ml water
    1 small onion, thinly sliced
    355ml strong coffee (instant works fine)
    1 tsp guar or xanthan

At least 24 to 36 hours before you want to actually cook your roast, stick holes
in the beef with a thin-bladed knife and insert a garlic slice into each hole. Put the
beef in a big bowl and pour the vinegar and the water over it. Put it in the refrigerator
and let it sit there for a day or so, turning it over when you think of it so the whole
thing marinates.

On the morning of the day you want to serve your roast, pour off the marinade and
put the beef in your slow cooker. Place the onion on top of the beef. Pour the coffee
over the beef and onion. Cover the slow cooker, set it to low, and let it cook for 8
hours for a smaller roast or up to 10 hours for a larger one.

When the time's up, remove the beef carefully from the cooker. (It will now be so
tender it's likely to fall apart.) Scoop out 450ml of the liquid and some of the onions
and put them in a blender with the guar or xanthan. Blend for few seconds, then
pour the mixture into a saucepan set over high heat. Boil this sauce hard for about
5 minutes to reduce it a bit. Add salt and pepper to the sauce to taste. (It's amazing
the difference the salt and pepper make here; I didn't like the flavour of this sauce
until I added the salt and pepper, and then I liked it a lot.) Slice the beef and serve
it with this sauce.

WARNING: Do not make this with a tender cut of beef! This recipe will tenderize the
toughest cut; a tender one will practically dissolve. Use inexpensive, tough cuts, and
prepare to be amazed at how fork-tender they get.

YIELD: 12 servings, each with: 324 calories, 24g fat, 24g protein, 3g carbohydrate,
trace dietary fibre, 3g usable carbs. (This analysis is for a 4-pound boneless roast.)

☕ Good Low-Carb slow-cooked Small Ribs

This was one of the first recipes I adapted from Peg Bracken's *I Hate To Cook Book*, aka The World's Funniest Cookbook (and also one of the most useful.) It was higher carb, and it wasn't originally a slow cooker recipe, but it adapted well to both!

225g tinned tomato sauce
175ml water
2 tbsps (30ml) wine or cider vinegar
4 tbsps (60ml) soy sauce
2 tsps Splenda
1.5–2kg beef small ribs
1 large onion, sliced
Guar or xanthan (optional)

In a bowl, mix together the tomato sauce, water, vinegar, soy sauce, and Splenda.

Put the ribs in your slow cooker. Place the onion on top of the ribs. Pour the sauce over the onion and ribs. Cover the slow cooker, set it to low, and let it cook for 8 to 9 hours. (If you put the ribs in thawed, cut about 1 hour off the cooking time.)

When the time's up, thicken the sauce with guar or xanthan if you prefer. (This recipe gives you tremendously tasty ribs in a thin but flavourful sauce – it's more like a stock. You can thicken it a bit with guar or xanthan, but I rather like it as it is.)

YIELD: 7 servings, each with: 559 calories, 31g fat, 61g protein, 5g carbohydrate, 1g dietary fibre, 4g usable carbs. (This analysis is for 1.4kg of ribs. The total carbs will vary with how much of the sauce you eat, because most of the carbs are in there. Furthermore, that calorie count assumes that you eat all of the fat that cooks off of the ribs – which I wouldn't suggest.)

CHAPTER FIVE

Slow Cooker Pork

This is one big chapter, and with good reason. Pork is delicious, nutritious, versatile, and slow cooks really well. You'll find everything from simple family suppers to company food in this chapter!

⏱ Braised Pork with Fennel

This was one of my first great slow-cooking triumphs, and it still ranks as one of the two or three best dishes I've ever cooked in my slow cooker. This is easily good enough to serve to company. Fennel looks like a bulb at the bottom, with celery-like stalks above, and feathery foliage. The stems are tough, but the foliage can be chopped up in salads or used as a garnish. It has a wonderful licorice-like taste.

2kg pork shoulder

2 tbsps (30ml) olive oil

1 medium onion, sliced

1 bulb fennel, sliced

235ml cider vinegar

3 tbsps (4.5g) Splenda

260g tinned chopped tomatoes, drained

235ml chicken stock

1 tsp chicken bouillon concentrate

2 cloves garlic, crushed

1/2 tsp dried thyme

1/2 tsp red pepper flakes, or to taste

Guar or xanthan

In a big, heavy frying pan, sear the pork in the oil over medium-high heat until it's brown all over. (This will take 20 minutes or so.) Transfer the pork to your slow cooker.

Pour off all but about 1 tbsp of fat from the frying pan and reduce the heat to medium-low. Sauté the onion and fennel until they're just getting a little golden. Transfer them to the slow cooker, too.

In a bowl, mix together the vinegar and Splenda. Pour the mixture over the pork. Add the tomatoes.

In a bowl, mix together the stock and bouillon until the bouillon dissolves. Stir in the garlic, thyme, and red pepper. Pour this over the pork, too. Cover the slow cooker, set it to low, and let it cook for 8 hours.

When the time's up, remove the pork from the slow cooker and place it on a serving dish. Using a slotted spoon, scoop out the vegetables and pile them around the pork. Cover the plate with foil and put it in a warm place.

Ladle the liquid from the slow cooker into a saucepan. Place it over the highest heat and boil it hard for 5 to 7 minutes, to reduce the sauce a bit. Add some guar or xanthan to thicken the sauce just a bit. (You want it to be about the texture of creamy milk, not a thick gravy.) Serve the sauce over the pork and vegetables.

YIELD: 6 servings, each with: 621 calories, 46g fat, 41g protein, 10g carbohydrate, 2g dietary fibre, 8g usable carbs.

⬚ Easy Pork Roast

This is basic, which is a strength, not a weakness. It would be a great supper with a big salad.

    1.5kg boneless pork loin
    2 tbsps (30ml) olive oil
    225g tomato sauce
    60ml soy sauce
    120ml chicken stock
    12g Splenda
    2 tsps dry mustard
    Guar or xanthan (optional)

In a big, heavy frying pan, brown the pork on all sides in the oil. Transfer the pork to your slow cooker.

In a bowl, mix together the tomato sauce, soy sauce, stock, Splenda, and dry mustard. Pour the mixture over the pork. Cover the slow cooker, set it to low, and let it cook for 8 to 9 hours.

When the time's up, remove the pork to a serving plate. Thicken the pot liquid, if needed, with guar or xanthan. Serve the juice with the pork.

YIELD: 8 servings, each with: 301 calories, 14g fat, 37g protein, 4g carbohydrate, 1g dietary fibre, 3g usable carbs.

Pork Roast with Apricot Sauce

Here's a fabulous Sunday dinner for the family – with very little work.

1.25kg boneless pork loin

2 tbsps (30ml) olive oil

35g chopped onion

175ml chicken stock

80g low-sugar apricot preserves

1 tbsp (15ml) balsamic vinegar

1 tbsp (15ml) lemon juice

1 tbsp (1.5g) Splenda

Guar or xanthan

In a big, heavy frying pan, sear the pork all over in the oil. Transfer the pork to your slow cooker. Scatter the onion around it.

In a bowl, mix together the stock, preserves, vinegar, lemon juice, and Splenda. Pour the mixture over the pork. Cover the slow cooker, set it to low, and let it cook for 7 hours.

When the time's up, remove the pork and put it on a serving plate. Season the juices with salt and pepper to taste. Thicken the juices with guar or xanthan. Ladle the juices into a sauce boat to serve.

YIELD: 6 servings, each with: 338 calories, 17g fat, 40g protein, 5g carbohydrate, trace dietary fibre, 5g usable carbs.

Pork Roast with Creamy Mushroom Gravy and Vegetables

Here's a great home-made dinner the family will love!

    1.25kg boneless pork loin
    60g sliced carrots
    115g sliced mushrooms
    280g frozen cross-cut green beans, unthawed
    1 tbsp (15ml) beef bouillon concentrate
    2 tbsps (30ml) water
    410g tinned tomatoes with roasted garlic
    Guar or xanthan
    120ml double cream

Put the pork in the bottom of your slow cooker. Surround the pork with the carrots, mushrooms, and green beans. (Don't bother thawing the green beans, just whack the bag hard on the counter before opening, so the beans are all separated.)

In a bowl, dissolve the bouillon in the water. Stir in the tomatoes. Pour the mixture over the pork and vegetables. Cover the slow cooker, set it to low, and let it cook for 8 to 9 hours.

When the time's up, remove the pork and vegetables to a serving dish. Thicken the juices in the pot with guar or xanthan, then whisk in the cream. Add salt and pepper to taste. Serve the juices with the pork and vegetables.

YIELD: 8 servings, each with: 284 calories, 19g fat, 23g protein, 5g carbohydrate, 1g dietary fibre, 4g usable carbs.

Orange Rosemary Pork

This modern citrus and herb combination really bring out the best in the pork!

 700g boneless pork loin
 30ml olive oil
 60ml white wine vinegar
 60ml lemon juice
 4.5g Splenda
 1/4 tsp orange extract
 1/2 tsp ground, dried rosemary
 1 clove garlic, crushed
 1 tsp soy sauce
 1/4 tsp pepper
 1/4 tsp salt or Vege-Sal

In a big, heavy frying pan, brown the pork in the oil over medium-high heat. Transfer the pork to your slow cooker.

In a bowl, stir together the vinegar, lemon juice, Splenda, orange extract, rosemary, garlic, soy sauce, pepper, and salt or Vege-Sal and pour over the pork. Cover the slow cooker, set it to low, and let it cook for 5 to 6 hours.

YIELD: 4 servings, each with: 317 calories, 23g fat, 23g protein, 3g carbohydrate, trace dietary fibre, 3g usable carbs.

⌂ Pork with Cabbage

Need I point out that this recipe is for cabbage lovers?

> 2kg boneless pork shoulder roast, trimmed of fat
>
> 2 tbsps (30ml) olive oil
>
> 2 carrots, cut into 3cm pieces
>
> 2 cloves garlic, crushed
>
> 2 stalks celery, cut 2cm thick
>
> 1 envelope (23g) onion soup mix
>
> 355ml water
>
> 700g cabbage, coarsely chopped
>
> Guar or xanthan

In a big, heavy frying pan, start browning the pork in the oil.

Place the carrots, garlic, and celery in your slow cooker. Add the soup mix and water.

When the pork is brown all over, put it on top of the vegetables in the slow cooker. Cover the slow cooker, set it to low, and let it cook for 7 hours.

When the time's up, stir in the cabbage, pushing it down into the liquid. Re-cover the slow cooker and let it cook for another 45 minutes to 1 hour

Remove the pork and put it on a serving dish. Use a slotted spoon to pile the vegetables around the pork. Thicken the liquid in the slow cooker with guar or xanthan. Add salt and pepper to taste. Pour the liquid into a sauce boat and serve with the pork and vegetables.

YIELD: 8 servings, each with: 478 calories, 35g fat, 31g protein, 10g carbohydrate, 3g dietary fibre, 7g usable carbs.

⏲ Pork with Swede

If you haven't tried swede, you simply must. Also sometimes called a 'yellow turnip', swede is similar to a turnip, except that it has an entrancing bitter-sweet flavour. Anyway, it's fun confusing supermarket checkout kids who can't figure out what that big yellow root is! It's actually delicious to make this with half swede and half a fresh, cubed pumpkin, but it's just not possible to find fresh pumpkin some seasons of the year.

> 1.25kg swede, peeled and cubed
>
> 1.5kg boneless pork shoulder roast, tied or netted
>
> 1/2 tsp black treacle
>
> 12g Splenda
>
> 1/4 tsp cayenne
>
> 1 clove garlic, finely chopped

Put the swede in the bottom of your slow cooker. Put the pork on top. Drizzle the treacle over the pork and swede.

In a bowl, mix together the Splenda, cayenne, and garlic. Sprinkle the mixture over the pork and swedez. Cover the slow cooker, set it to low, and let it cook for 8 to 9 hours.

When the time's up, remove the pork from the slow cooker, cut off the string or net, and slice or pull the pork apart. Serve the pork over the rutabaga with the pot liquid.

YIELD: 6 servings, each with: 472 calories, 31g fat, 32g protein, 16g carbohydrate, 5g dietary fibre, 11g usable carbs.

🝜 'Honey' Mustard Ham

You may wonder how to roast a ham when you're not going to be around for hours to tend the oven. In your slow cooker, of course. You'll need a big slow cooker for this.

> 2.5kg fully cooked, bone-in ham
> 75ml apple cider vinegar
> 12g Splenda
> 1 tbsp (15g) brown mustard
> 1/2 tsp black treacle
> 1 tsp water

Place the ham in your slow cooker.

In a bowl, mix together the vinegar and 2 tbsps of the Splenda. Add the mixture to the slow cooker. In the same bowl, mix together the mustard, treacle, remaining Splenda, and water and spread the mixture over the ham. Cover the slow cooker, set it to low, and let it cook for 7 hours.

YIELD: 6 servings, each with: 683 calories, 41g fat, 68g protein, 6g carbohydrate, trace dietary fibre, 6g usable carbs.

⌂ Ham with Swede and Turnips

If you're roasting a ham in your slow cooker, you may as well roast your vegetables, too, right?

> 4 turnips, cubed
>
> 700g swede, peeled and cubed
>
> 3.25kg shank half ham

Put the turnips and swede in the bottom of your slow cooker. Place the ham on top, flat side down. Cover the slow cooker, set it to low, and let it cook for 5 to 6 hours. Again, you'll need a big slow cooker.

YIELD: 10 servings, each with: 674 calories, 51g fat, 43g protein, 9g carbohydrate, 3g dietary fibre, 6g usable carbs.

Creamy Ham Casserole

I made this up to use the end of a ham I'd slow cooked, and it was a hit with my husband.

 1 head cauliflower
 1 medium onion, chopped
 1 large stalk celery, with leaves
 475ml semi-skimmed milk
 235ml chicken stock
 6 tsps guar or xanthan
 1 tsp dry mustard
 1 tsp salt or Vege-Sal
 1/2 tsp pepper
 225g Gruyère cheese, grated

Run the cauliflower through the slicing blade of your food processor. Transfer it to a bowl and replace the slicing disc with the S-blade. Chop the onion and celery fine in the food processor.

With a hand blender or regular blender, blend the milk and stock. Add the guar or xanthan and blend it until there are no lumps. Pour the mixture it into a saucepan and heat it over medium-low heat. (If you do have a hand blender, you may as well just dump the milk and the chicken stock in the saucepan and use the hand blender to blend in the thickener in the pot to save a little dishwashing.) Stir in the dry mustard, salt or Vege-Sal, and pepper. When the sauce is hot, stir in the cheese, a little at a time, until it's all melted. Turn off the burner.

Spray your slow cooker with oil to prevent sticking. Put in a layer of cauliflower, a lighter layer of onion and celery, then a generous layer of ham. Repeat these layers until everything's gone and the slow cooker is full. Pour half of the sauce over the top. It won't immediately flow down into the food in the slow cooker, so poke down into it several times with the handle of a rubber scraper or spoon, piercing the layers to the bottom. The sauce will start to seep down. When there's more room on top, pour in the rest of the sauce, and poke down through the layers again. Cover the slow cooker, set it to low, and let it cook for 6 to 7 hours.

YIELD: 8 servings, each with: 287 calories, 19g fat, 24g protein, 5g carbohydrate, 1g dietary fibre, 4g usable carbs.

⊡ Sweet and Sour Pork

Here's another stir-fry dish turned into a slow cooker meal. This lacks the chunks of pineapple you often find in sweet-and-sour dishes. They're just too high carb. But the crushed pineapple in the sauce gives the right flavour!

> 700g boneless pork loin, cut into 3cm cubes
>
> 1 green bell pepper, diced
>
> Splenda
>
> 1 tbsp (8g) grated ginger root
>
> 1 clove garlic, crushed
>
> 60ml rice vinegar
>
> 3 tbsps (45ml) soy sauce
>
> 1/4 tsp black treacle
>
> 65g tinned crushed pineapple in juice
>
> 1/2 head cauliflower
>
> Guar or xanthan

Put the pork and pepper in your slow cooker.

In a bowl, mix together the Splenda, ginger, garlic, vinegar, soy sauce, treacle, and pineapple. Pour the mixture over the pork and pepper. Cover the slow cooker, set it on low, and let it cook for 6 hours.

When the time's up, run the cauliflower through the shredding blade of a food processor and put it in a microwaveable casserole dish with a lid. Add a couple of tbsps of water, cover, and microwave on high for 7 minutes. This is your Cauli-Rice!

Meanwhile, thicken up the pot juices with guar or xanthan until they're about the texture of commercial Chinese food. Serve the pork mixture over the Cauli-Rice.

YIELD: 4 servings, each with: 283 calories, 11g fat, 36g protein, 9g carbohydrate, 1g dietary fibre, 8g usable carbs.

☐ Curried Pork Stew

This is not terribly authentic, but it's awfully good. Try one of the chutneys (see recipe pages 208 and 210) with this.

> 450g boneless pork loin, cubed
> 1/2 tsp salt
> 2 tbsps (12g) curry powder
> 1 tbsp (15ml) olive oil
> 1 onion, sliced
> 2 small turnips, cubed
> 260g tinned chopped tomatoes
> 120ml cider vinegar
> 2 tbsps (3g) Splenda
> 300g diced cauliflower

Season the pork with the salt and sprinkle with 1 tbsp of the curry powder.

In a big, heavy frying pan, heat the oil and brown the pork over medium-high heat.

Place the onion and turnips in your slow cooker. Top with the pork and tomatoes.

In a bowl, stir together the vinegar, Splenda, and the remaining 1 tbsp curry powder. Pour the mixture over the pork. Cover the slow cooker, set it to low, and let it cook for 7 hours.

When the time's up, stir in the cauliflower. Re-cover the slow cooker and cook for 1 more hour, or until the cauliflower is tender.

YIELD: 6 servings, each with: 177 calories, 8g fat, 17g protein, 11g carbohydrate, 3g dietary fibre, 8g usable carbs.

Pork and 'Apple' Stew

The apple flavour here comes from the apple cider vinegar. Our tester, Maria, cut her turnips into apple-slice shapes, and her family thought they were apples! They loved the whole thing.

> 1kg pork loin, cut into 1' cubes
> 2 medium turnips, cubed
> 2 medium carrots, cut 2cm thick
> 1 medium onion, sliced
> 60g sliced celery
> 235ml apple cider vinegar
> 3 tbsps (4.5g) Splenda
> 235ml chicken stock
> 1 tsp chicken bouillon concentrate
> 1 tsp caraway seeds
> 1/4 tsp pepper

Combine the pork, turnips, carrots, onion, and celery in your slow cooker.

In a bowl, stir together the vinegar, Splenda, stock, and bouillon. Pour the mixture over the pork and vegetables. Add the caraway seeds and pepper and stir everything. Cover the slow cooker, set it to low, and let it cook for 8 hours.

YIELD: 6 servings, each with: 226 calories, 6g fat, 34g protein, 10g carbohydrate, 2g dietary fibre, 8g usable carbs.

Easy Southwestern Pork Stew

Our tester gave this a 10 – and so did her family!

1 medium onion, chopped

3 cloves garlic, crushed

1kg boneless pork loin, cut into 1' cubes

2 tsps ground cumin

1 tbsp (4g) dried oregano

1/2 tsp salt

425g tinned black soybeans

410g tinned tomatoes with green chillies

235ml chicken stock

1 tsp chicken bouillon concentrate

Put the onion and garlic in your slow cooker and place the pork on top.

In a bowl, stir together the cumin, oregano, salt, soybeans, tomatoes, stock, and bouillon. Pour the mixture over the pork and vegetables. Cover the slow cooker, set it to low, and let it cook for 8 to 9 hours.

YIELD: 6 servings, each with: 257 calories, 10g fat, 34g protein, 6g carbohydrate, 1g dietary fibre, 5g usable carbs.

Orange Pork Loin

Boneless pork loin frequently goes on sale. It's very lean, however, so it's often both bland and dry. Slow cooking takes care of that little problem! Sadly, fresh pumpkin is only available for a couple of months in the autumn, so that's when you'll need to make this dish. Buy a small pumpkin, or you'll have piles of it left over.

450g pumpkin, peeled and cut into 2cm cubes

450g swede, cut into 2cm cubes

2 tbsps (30ml) olive oil

1kg pork loin

2 tbsps (40g) low-sugar marmalade or orange preserves

1/4 tsp orange extract

2 tsps Splenda

2 cloves garlic, crushed

1/2 tsp salt

120ml chicken stock

Guar or xanthan

Put the pumpkin and swede in the bottom of your slow cooker.

In a big, heavy frying pan, heat the oil over medium-high heat and brown the pork all over. Put the pork in the slow cooker on top of the pumpkin and swede.

In a bowl, stir together the marmalade, orange extract, Splenda, garlic, salt, and stock. Pour the mixture over the pork. Cover the slow cooker, set it to low, and let it cook for 8 hours.

When the time's up, carefully remove the pork to a serving dish and use a slotted spoon to pile the vegetables around it. Use guar or xanthan to thicken the liquid in the pot to the consistency of double cream. Serve the liquid with the pork and vegetables.

YIELD: 6 servings, each with: 281 calories, 10g fat, 34g protein, 13g carbohydrate, 2g dietary fibre, 11g usable carbs.

Pork Slow Cooker Chilli

Try this when you want to have people over after the kids' football game!

    1 tbsp (15ml) olive oil
    1.25kg boneless pork loin, cut into 2cm cubes
    410g tinned tomatoes with green chillies
    25g chopped onion
    30g diced green bell pepper
    1 clove garlic, crushed
    1 tbsp (7g) chilli powder

In a big, heavy frying pan, heat the oil and brown the pork all over. Transfer the pork to your slow cooker. Stir in the tomatoes, onion, pepper, garlic, and chilli powder. Cover the slow cooker, set it to low, and let it cook for 6 to 8 hours.

Serve this with sour cream and grated Gouda cheese, if you like, but it's darned good as is.

YIELD: 8 servings, each with: 189 calories, 8g fat, 25g protein, 3g carbohydrate, 1g dietary fibre, 2g usable carbs.

⊡ Slow Cooker Mu Shu Pork

This isn't authentic, by any means, but it's very tasty. My husband, not a big Chinese food guy, really liked this.

    2 plums, pitted and chopped
    1 clove garlic, crushed
    2 tbsps (16g) grated ginger root
    60ml soy sauce
    2 tbsps (30ml) dry sherry
    2 tsps dark sesame oil
    1/8 tsp five-spice powder
    1 tbsp (15ml) rice vinegar
    3 tbsps (4.5g) Splenda
    1kg boneless pork loin,
        cut into a few big chunks across the grain
    Guar or xanthan
    5 eggs, beaten
    100g bean sprouts
    140g shredded cabbage
    16 6-inch low-carb tortillas
    75g sliced spring onions
    Hoisin Sauce (optional, see recipe page 233)

Put the plums, garlic, ginger, soy sauce, sherry, sesame oil, five-spice powder, vinegar, and Splenda in a food processor with the S-blade in place and run until the plum is pureed.

Place the pork in your slow cooker. Pour the plum sauce over the pork. Cover the slow cooker, set it to low, and let it cook for 7 to 8 hours.

When the time's up, scoop out the pork with a slotted spoon and put it on a big plate. Use a couple of forks to tear the pork into little shreds. Thicken the sauce in the slow cooker to about ketchup consistency with guar or xanthan. Stir the shredded pork back into the slow cooker. Re-cover the slow cooker, set it to high, and let it cook for 30 minutes.

Meanwhile, spray a big, heavy frying pan well with oil to prevent sticking. (A nonstick frying pan is even better for this.) Put it over medium-high heat and let it get hot. Pour in enough of the eggs to form a thin layer on the bottom, and let it cook, not stirring, until it's a solid sheet. Lift the eggs out and set them on a plate. Cook the rest of the eggs into a thin sheet, as well. Use a sharp knife to cut these sheets of cooked egg into strips about 5mm wide. Reserve.

When the 30 minutes are up, stir the bean sprouts, cabbage, and finely chopped eggs into the pork mixture. Re-cover the slow cooker and let it cook for just another 10 to 15 minutes. (You want the bean sprouts to be hot through, but still have some crispness.) While that's happening, slice your spring onions. (If you're not going to be eating all of this right away, only slice enough spring onions for immediate use.)

To serve, spread some of the pork-and-egg-and-vegetable mixture on a tortilla, sprinkle with sliced spring onions, wrap, and eat! If you want to be more authentic, you could spread a little Hoisin Sauce on each tortilla before filling, but it's hardly essential.

YIELD: 16 servings, each with: 175 calories, 8g fat, 19g protein, 14g carbohydrate, 9g dietary fibre, 5g usable carbs.

Hot Asian Ribs

This is full-bodied Chinese flavour. If your family loves Chinese spare ribs, you have to make this!

1.75kg country-style pork ribs
4 spring onions, sliced
60ml soy sauce
8g Splenda
1 tsp black treacle
2 tbsps (30ml) white wine vinegar
2 tsps toasted sesame oil
2 tsps lemon juice
1/2 tsp hot sauce
1 clove garlic
1/2 tsp ground ginger
1/2 tsp chilli powder
1/4 tsp red pepper flakes
6 tsps Hoisin Sauce (see recipe page 233)

Put the ribs in your slow cooker.

In a bowl, mix together the spring onions, soy sauce, Splenda, treacle, vinegar, sesame oil, lemon juice, hot sauce, garlic, ginger, chilli powder, red pepper flakes, and Hoisin Sauce. Pour the sauce over the ribs. Cover the slow cooker, set it to low, and let it cook for 8 to 9 hours.

YIELD: 6 servings, each with: 469 calories, 35g fat, 32g protein, 4g carbohydrate, 1g dietary fibre, 3g usable carbs.

Key West Ribs

The citrusy barbeque sauce gives this a Florida kind of taste!

   1.5kg country-style pork ribs
   30g finely chopped onion
   60ml low-carb barbeque sauce
      (recipe from page 231 or purchased)
   1 tsp grated orange peel
   1 tsp grated lemon peel
   1/2 tsp salt
   2 tbsps (30ml) white wine vinegar
   2 tbsps (30ml) lemon juice
   2 tbsps (30ml) lime juice
   1 1/2 tbsps (2g) Splenda
   1/8 tsp orange extract
   2 tbsps (30ml) olive oil

In a big, heavy frying pan, brown the ribs over medium-high heat. Transfer them to your slow cooker.

In a bowl, mix together the onion, barbeque sauce, orange peel, lemon rind, salt, vinegar, lemon juice, lime juice, Splenda, orange extract, and oil. Pour the mixture over the ribs. Cover the slow cooker, set it to low, and let it cook for 7 to 9 hours.

Serve the ribs together with the sauce.

YIELD: 6 servings, each with: 421 calories, 33g fat, 26g protein, 3g carbohydrate, trace dietary fibre, 3g usable carbs.

Maple-Spice Country-Style Ribs

My pal Ray Stevens, who has tested many recipes for me, raves about this. It's shaping up to be the recipe by which all other recipes are judged!

    1.5kg meaty pork ribs
    120ml sugar-free pancake syrup
    3 tbsps (4.5g) Splenda
    2 tbsps (30ml) soy sauce
    25g chopped onion
    1/2 tsp ground cinnamon
    1/2 tsp ground ginger
    1/2 tsp ground allspice
    3 cloves garlic, crushed
    1/4 tsp pepper
    1/8 tsp cayenne

Put the ribs in your slow cooker.

In a bowl, mix together the syrup, Splenda, soy sauce, onion, cinnamon, ginger, allspice, garlic, pepper, and cayenne. Pour the mixture over the ribs. Cover the slow cooker, set it to low, and let it cook for 9 hours.

YIELD: 6 servings, each with: 382 calories, 29g fat, 27g protein, 2g carbohydrate, trace dietary fibre, 2g usable carbs.

Orange-Glazed Country Ribs

Fruit flavours of all kinds bring out the best in pork.

1kg meaty pork ribs

1/2 small onion, sliced

1 clove garlic, crushed

7g butter

60g finely chopped green bell pepper

1/2 clove garlic, crushed

3 tbsps (60g) low-sugar orange marmalade

60ml lemon juice

1 tbsp (1.5g) Splenda

1/4 tsp orange extract

1 tbsp (8g) grated ginger root

Guar or xanthan

Spray your slow cooker with oil to prevent sticking. Add the ribs, onion, and garlic. Cover the slow cooker, set it to low, and let it cook for 7 to 8 hours.

When the time's up, melt the butter in a medium-size nonstick saucepan. Add the pepper and garlic and sauté until it's just soft. Add the marmalade, lemon juice, Splenda, orange extract, and ginger, bring to a simmer, and let it cook for 5 minutes. Thicken the sauce a little with guar or xanthan.

Remove the ribs from the slow cooker and put them on a grill rack. Brush them with the sauce and run them under the grill, set on high, for 5 minutes to glaze. Serve with the rest of the sauce.

YIELD: 6 servings, each with: 304 calories, 20g fat, 27g protein, 3g carbohydrate, trace dietary fibre, 3g usable carbs.

☺ Ribs 'n' Kraut

If you like, you can make this with smoked sausage instead of the ribs.
If you do, read the labels to find the lowest carb smoked sausage.

> 1kg meaty pork ribs
> 1 medium Granny Smith apple, diced
> 1/2 medium onion, sliced
> 450g sauerkraut, rinsed and drained
> 3 tbsps (4.5g) Splenda
> 1/2 tsp black treacle
> 1 tsp caraway seeds
> 60ml dry white wine

Put the ribs, apple, and onion in your slow cooker. Cover with the sauerkraut.

In a bowl, stir together the Splenda, treacle, caraway seeds, and wine. Pour the
mixture over the sauerkraut and ribs. Cover the slow cooker, set it to low, and let it
cook for 8 hours.

YIELD: 6 servings, each with: 286 calories, 19g fat, 18g protein, 7g carbohydrate,
3g dietary fibre, 4g usable carbs.

⬚ Ribs with Apple Kraut

Even folks who aren't wild about sauerkraut may like this. With the apple and the other vegetables, there's a lot more than just sauerkraut going on here.

> 1.75kg meaty pork ribs
> 2 tbsps (30ml) oil
> 110g diced cauliflower
> 110g diced turnip
> 1 Granny Smith apple, cored and thinly sliced
> 2 carrots, sliced
> 1 medium onion, sliced
> 450g sauerkraut, rinsed and drained
> 120ml apple cider vinegar
> 3 tbsps (4.5g) Splenda
> 2 tsps caraway seeds
> 1/8 tsp ground cloves
> Guar or xanthan

In a big, heavy frying pan, brown the ribs in the oil over medium-high heat.

Put the cauliflower, turnip, apple, carrots, and onion in your slow cooker. Put the ribs and sauerkraut on top.

In a bowl, mix together the vinegar, Splenda, caraway seeds, and cloves. Pour the mixture over the ribs and sauerkraut. Cover the slow cooker, set it to low, and let it cook for 8 to 9 hours.

When the time's up, remove the ribs to a serving dish with tongs and scoop out the vegetables with a slotted spoon. Thicken the pot liquid with guar or xanthan, add salt and pepper to taste, and serve the sauce with the ribs and vegetables.

YIELD: 6 servings, each with: 529 calories, 39g fat, 32g protein, 13g carbohydrate, 4g dietary fibre, 9g usable carbs.

Slow Cooker Barbeque

This is simple, simple, simple.

> 2 tbsps (12g) Classic Rub (see recipe page 234)
> or prepared spice rub
> 1.25kg pork spareribs, cut into 2 or 3 pieces
> to fit into your slow cooker
> 75ml Dana's 'Kansas City' Barbeque Sauce
> (see recipe page 231) or purchased low-carb barbeque sauce

Sprinkle 1 tbsp of rub over each side of the ribs. Put the ribs on a grill rack and grill them on high, about 15cm from the heat, for about 5 to 7 minutes per side, or until well browned. Transfer the ribs to your slow cooker.

Pour the barbeque sauce evenly over the ribs and use a spoon to spread it, so the 'up' side of the ribs is coated. Cover the slow cooker, set it to low, and let it cook for 6 hours.

YIELD: 3 servings, each with: 688 calories, 56g fat, 40g protein, 4g carbohydrate, trace dietary fibre, 4g usable carbs.

Polynesian Pork Ribs

It's a luau in your slow cooker!

> 1kg country-style pork ribs
> 1 clove garlic, crushed
> 1/2 medium onion, sliced
> 50g tinned crushed pineapple in juice
> 120g Dana's No-Sugar Ketchup (see recipe page 228)
>   or purchased low-carb ketchup
> 1 tbsp (1.5g) Splenda
> 1/2 tsp black treacle
> 1 tbsp (15ml) soy sauce
> 1 tsp grated ginger root
> 1/2 tsp dark sesame oil
> 1 tbsp (15ml) cider vinegar

Put the ribs in your slow cooker, along with the garlic and onion.

In a bowl, stir together the pineapple and half of the ketchup. Pour the mixture over the ribs. Cover the slow cooker, set it to low, and let it cook for 8 to 10 hours.

When the time's up, pull the ribs out of the slow cooker, put them on a grill rack, and stash them somewhere warm.

Ladle the cooking liquid into a saucepan. Stir in the remaining 1/4 cup ketchup, the Splenda, treacle, soy sauce, ginger, sesame oil, and vinegar, bring to a simmer, and let cook until you have a passably thick sauce.

Spoon the sauce over the ribs and run them under the grill for 5 minutes or so, just to glaze them a bit.

YIELD: 6 servings, each with: 288 calories, 20g fat, 19g protein, 9g carbohydrate, 1g dietary fibre, 8g usable carbs.

⌂ Soy and Sesame Ribs

Here's another Asian take on ribs. The toasted sesame seed topping really sets this recipe apart.

    1.5kg pork spareribs
    8g Splenda
    60g Dana's No-Sugar Ketchup (see recipe page 228)
        or prepared low-carb ketchup
    1 tbsp (20g) sugar-free imitation honey
    1 tbsp (30ml) cider vinegar
    1 clove garlic, crushed
    1/2 tsp ground ginger
    1/2 tsp red pepper flakes
    1/2 tsp dark sesame oil
    1 tbsp (8g) sesame seeds
    4 spring onions, thinly sliced

Cut the ribs into portions if needed to fit them in your slow cooker. Grill the ribs about 16cm from high heat until browned, about 10 minutes per side. Transfer them to your slow cooker.

In a bowl, mix together the Splenda, ketchup, honey, vinegar, garlic, ginger, red pepper, and sesame oil. Pour the mixture over the ribs, turning to coat if needed. Cover the slow cooker, set it to low, and let it cook for 5 to 6 hours.

Toast the sesame seeds by stirring them in a dry frying pan over medium-high heat until they start to make popping sounds and jump around a bit. Serve the ribs with sesame seeds and spring onions scattered over them.

YIELD: 4 servings, each with: 646 calories, 52g fat, 37g protein, 7g carbohydrate, 1g dietary fibre, 6g usable carbs. (Counts do not include the polyols in the imitation honey.)

Teriyaki-Tangerine Ribs

This is an easy twist on plain old teriyaki.

> 2kg meaty pork ribs
> Teriyaki Sauce (see recipe page 233)
> Florida Sunshine Tangerine Barbeque Sauce (see recipe page 230)

Put the ribs in your slow cooker.

In a bowl, mix together the Teriyaki Sauce and the Florida Sunshine Tangerine Barbeque Sauce. Pour the mixture over the ribs. Cover the slow cooker, set it to low, and let it cook for 7 to 8 hours.

When the time's up, remove the ribs. Transfer the sauce to a nonstick saucepan and put it over high heat. Boil it hard until it thickens up a bit and serve the sauce over the ribs.

YIELD: 8 servings, each with: 415 calories, 29g fat, 28g protein, 8g carbohydrate, 1g dietary fibre, 7g usable carbs.

⎕ Slow Cooker Pulled Pork

Pulled pork is a Carolina tradition, and it usually involves many, many hours of long, slow smoking. This is not authentic, but it is tasty, and thanks to liquid smoke flavouring, it has an appealingly smoky flavour. This recipe requires a meat injector, a big, scary-looking syringe that looks like your doctor got way out of hand. You can buy inexpensive ones at housewares stores.

> 75ml liquid smoke flavouring (for this specialist ingredient,
>   try www.uniqueingredients.co.uk)
> 1.5kg pork shoulder
> Sauces, such as Eastern Carolina Vinegar Sauce (see recipe page 232),
>   Dana's 'Kansas City' Barbeque Sauce (see recipe page 231),
>   and Piedmont Mustard Sauce (see recipe page 232)

Slurp up a syringe-full of the liquid smoke flavouring and inject it into a dozen sites all over the pork shoulder. Season the pork with salt and pepper. Place the pork in your slow cooker and pour another tbsp or two of liquid smoke over it. Cover the slow cooker, set it to low, and let it cook for 8 hours.

When the time's up, remove the pork from the slow cooker and pull out the bone, which will be very easy to do at this point. Discard the bone, along with any surface fat. Use two forks to pull the meat into shreds. Toss it with one of the sauces.

You can serve Pulled Pork in one of a few ways: You can wrap it in low-carb tortillas, serve it on low-carb buns, or, my favourite, serve it on a bed of coleslaw.

YIELD: 6 servings, each with: 405 calories, 31g fat, 29g protein, trace carbohydrate, trace dietary fibre, 0g usable carbs.

Slow Cooker Teriyaki Ribs

This dish is sweet, spicy, and tangy, and falling-off-the-bone tender

3kg pork spareribs, cut into 3 or 4 pieces so they fit in the slow cooker

180g Dana's No-Sugar Ketchup (see recipe page 228)

   or purchased low-carb ketchup

1 batch Teriyaki Sauce (see recipe page 233)

6g Splenda

1/4 tsp black treacle

1 tsp finely chopped garlic or 2 cloves garlic, crushed

Guar or xanthan

Place the ribs in your slow cooker.

In a bowl, mix the ketchup, Teriyaki Sauce, Splenda, treacle, and garlic together. Pour the mixture over the ribs. Cover the slow cooker, set it to low, and let it cook for 10 hours.

When the time's up, use tongs to pull out the now unbelievably tender and flavourful ribs. Ladle out as much of the pot liquid as you think you'll use and thicken it using guar or xanthan. Serve the sauce over the ribs.

YIELD: 8 servings, each with: 650 calories, 50g fat, 38g protein, 9g carbohydrate, 1g dietary fibre (depending on how much of the liquid you eat), about 8g usable carbs.

⊙ Fruity, Spicy Ribs

This recipe is a little hot, a little sweet, a little Southwestern, and a little Asian – but all tasty.

> 3kg pork spareribs, cut in pieces so they fit in your slow cooker
> 120g low-sugar apricot preserves
> 75ml lemon juice
> 2 tbsps (3g) Splenda
> 2 tbsps (15g) chilli powder
> 2 tsps five-spice powder
> 60ml soy sauce
> 120ml chicken stock

Put the ribs on a grill rack and grill them about 6' (15cm from high heat for about 7 to 8 minutes per side, or until browned. Transfer the ribs to your slow cooker.

In a bowl, mix together the preserves, lemon juice, Splenda, chilli powder, five-spice powder, soy sauce, and stock. Pour the mixture over the ribs. Cover the slow cooker, set it to low, and let it cook for 6 to 7 hours.

When the time's up, remove the ribs to a serving dish. Pour off the liquid in the pot into a deep, clear container, and let the fat rise to the top. Skim off the fat. Now pour the liquid into a saucepan. Boil it hard until it's reduced by at least half and starting to thicken. Serve the sauce with the ribs.

YIELD: 8 servings, each with: 636 calories, 50g fat, 37g protein, 7g carbohydrate, 1g dietary fibre, 6g usable carbs.

⏱ Rosemary–Ginger Ribs with Apricot Glaze

This recipe originally appeared in *15-Minute Low-Carb Recipes*. Feel free to use a full-size slab of ribs – about 3kg worth – and double the seasonings if you're feeding a family.

> 1 slab back ribs, about 1kg
> Rosemary-ginger spice
> 40g low-sugar apricot preserves
> 1 1/2 tsps spicy brown mustard
> 1 tsp Splenda
> 1 1/2 tsps soy sauce

Sprinkle both sides of the ribs generously with the rosemary-ginger rub. Curl the slab of ribs around and fit it down into your slow cooker. Cover the slow cooker, set it to low, and let it cook for 9 to 10 hours. (No, I didn't forget anything. You don't put any liquid in the slow cooker. Don't fret.)

When the time's up, mix together the preserves, mustard, Splenda, and soy sauce. Carefully remove the ribs from the slow cooker. (They may fall apart on you a bit because they'll be so tender.) Arrange the ribs meaty-side-up on a grill rack. Spread the apricot glaze evenly over the ribs and run them under a grill set on high, 7 to 10cm from the heat, for 7 to 8 minutes.

YIELD: 3 servings, each with: 689 calories, 56g fat, 40g protein, 4g carbohydrate, trace dietary fibre, 4g usable carbs.

⛭ Slow Cooker 'Barbequed' Ribs

Okay, it's not really barbeque because it's not done over a fire. But this recipe tastes great and lets you dig into your ribs within minutes of walking through the door.

> 1kg pork spare ribs
> 2 tbsp (15g) Classic Rub (see recipe page 234) or purchased seasoning
> 150ml Dana's 'Kansas City' Barbeque Sauce
>   (see recipe page 231) or purchased low-carb barbeque sauce

Sprinkle the slab of ribs liberally on both sides with the seasoning, coil the ribs up, and slide them into your slow cooker. Cover the slow cooker, set it to low, and let it cook for 9 to 10 hours.

When the time's up, pull the ribs out of the slow cooker. (Do this carefully because they'll be tender and falling apart.) Lay the ribs on a grill rack, meaty-side-up, and spread the barbeque sauce over them. Grill 7 to 10cm from the grill set on high for 7 to 8 minutes.

NOTE: If you'd like to give these a smoked flavour, you can buy liquid smoke flavouring online, try www.uniqueingredients.co.uk. Simply brush the ribs with the liquid smoke before you sprinkle on the seasoning.

YIELD: 3 servings, each with: 688 calories, 56g fat, 40g protein, 4g carbohydrate, 1g dietary fibre, 3g usable carbs. (Your carb count will be a bit different depending on whether you use homemade sugar-free barbeque sauce or commercial low-carb sauce.)

About Pork Neckbones

Unless you grew up on soul food, you may never have tried pork neckbones. They're another one of those cuts that are perfect for the slow cooker. They're bony and tough, and cheap. Yet cooked with slow moist heat, they're incredibly flavourful, and because the meat falls right off the bone, who cares that they're bony?

I did have one teeny problem with pork neckbones: I simply could not find any nutritional statistics for them, and I even wrote to a big pork producer! However, you can count on them being carb-free, so these carb counts are accurate. It's the protein and calorie counts that I couldn't get, so that's why they're missing in these neckbone recipes.

⊡ Stewed Pork Neckbones with Turnips and Cabbage

This one-pot meal is not a beautiful dish to look at, but boy, does it taste good! Plenty of Tabasco is essential.

> 3 turnips, diced
> 1.5kg meaty pork neckbones
> 1 tsp red pepper flakes
> 1 1/2 tsps salt or Vege-Sal
> 700ml water
> 1/2 head cabbage, cut in wedges
> Tabasco sauce

Put the turnips in the bottom of your slow cooker. Put the neckbones on top of them. Sprinkle the red pepper and salt or Vege-Sal over it, then pour the water over that. Now arrange the cabbage wedges on top of that. Cover the slow cooker, set it to low, and let it cook for 7 to 8 hours.

Scoop everything out onto a serving dish together with a slotted spoon and dose it well with Tabasco sauce before serving.

YIELD: 4 servings, each with: 6g carbohydrate, 2g dietary fibre, 4g usable carbs.

Neckbones and 'Rice'

I adapted this recipe from one on a soul food website. I have no experience with genuine soul food, so I can't tell you how close this comes, but it's great in its own right.

1.25kg meaty pork neckbones
120ml oil
1 medium onion, sliced
1 tbsp (9g) garlic powder
1 tsp salt or Vege-Sal
1 tsp pepper
475ml chicken stock
1/2 head cauliflower
Guar or xanthan

In a big, heavy frying pan, brown the pork neckbones in the oil over medium-high heat, in batches. Transfer the neckbones to your slow cooker.

Add the onion and sprinkle the garlic powder, salt or Vege-Sal, and pepper over the whole thing. Pour in the stock and give the whole thing a stir. Cover the slow cooker, set it to low, and let it cook for 6 to 7 hours.

When the time's up, run the cauliflower through the shredding blade of a food processor. Put the resulting Cauli-Rice in a microwaveable casserole dish with a lid. Add a couple of tbsps of water, cover, and microwave on high for 7 minutes.

Meanwhile, remove the neckbones to a serving dish. Thicken the liquid a little with guar or xanthan. Serve the neckbones, onions, and gravy over the Cauli-Rice.

YIELD: 3 servings, each with: 7g carbohydrate, 1g dietary fibre, 6g usable carbs.

⛾ Cocido de Puerco

This pork stew appeared in *500 Low-Carb Recipes*, but I hadn't thought of slow cooking it yet. It worked out great!

  1.5kg pork neckbones
  2 tbsps (30ml) olive oil
  1 small onion, chopped
  1 clove garlic, crushed
  1 green bell pepper, diced
  2 medium courgette, chunked
  410g tinned chopped tomatoes
  2 tsps cumin
  2 tsps dried oregano
  1/2 tsp red pepper flakes
  1 large onion, sliced

In a big, heavy frying pan, brown the pork neckbones in the oil.

While that's happening, put the onion and garlic in the bottom of your slow cooker. When the neckbones are browned, put them in the slow cooker on top of the onions. Put the pepper and courgette on top.

In a bowl, stir together the tomatoes, cumin, oregano, and red pepper. Pour the mixture into the slow cooker. Cover the slow cooker, set it to low, and let it cook for 6 to 7 hours.

YIELD: 5 servings, each with: 12g carbohydrate, 2g dietary fibre, 10g usable carbs.

Stuffed Peppers

        6 large green peppers

        700g bulk Italian sausage

        1/2 head cauliflower

        500g no-sugar-added spaghetti sauce

        110g crumbled feta cheese

        50g chopped onion

        40g chopped tomato

        16g chopped fresh parsley

        2 tbsps (12g) chopped black olives

        1 clove garlic, crushed

        1/2 tsp salt or Vege-Sal

        1 tsp Italian seasoning

        1/2 tsp red pepper flakes

Cut the tops off the peppers. Remove the usable pepper wall from the stems and chop it, discarding the stems and seeds. Reserve the pepper shells.

In a big, heavy frying pan, brown and crumble the sausage till done. Drain the fat.

Run the cauliflower through the shredding blade of a food processor. Place the resulting Cauli-Rice in a big mixing bowl.

Put 1 cup of the spaghetti sauce in the slow cooker. Add the rest to the Cauli-Rice. Add the cheese, onion, tomato, parsley, olives, garlic, salt or Vege-Sal, Italian seasoning, red pepper, cooked sausage, and the chopped bit of green pepper to the Cauli-Rice. Combine well. Divide the mixture between the pepper shells.

Put the stuffed peppers in the slow cooker. Cover the slow cooker, set it to low, and let it cook for 4 to 5 hours, or until the peppers are tender.

YIELD: 6 servings, each with: 592 calories, 51g fat, 18g protein, 18g carbohydrate, 5g dietary fibre, 13g usable carbs.

⌂ Tangy Pork Chops

2kg pork chops, 2cm thick

1/2 tsp salt or Vege-Sal

1/4 tsp pepper

50g chopped onion

2 stalks celery, diced

1 green bell pepper, diced

410g tinned chopped tomatoes

120g Dana's No-Sugar Ketchup (see recipe page 228)
    or purchased low-carb ketchup

2 tbsps (30ml) cider vinegar

2 tbsps (30g) Worcestershire sauce

2 tbsps (3g) Splenda

1/4 tsp black molasses

1 tbsp (15ml) lemon juice

1 tsp beef bouillon concentrate

Guar or xanthan

Place the pork in the bottom of your slow cooker. Sprinkle the pork with the salt and pepper. Now add the onion, celery, green pepper, and tomatoes.

In a bowl, stir together the ketchup, vinegar, Worcestershire sauce, Splenda, treacle, lemon juice, and bouillon. Stir until the bouillon dissolves. Pour the mixture into the slow cooker. Cover the slow cooker, set it to low, and let it cook for 5 to 6 hours.

When the time's up, remove the pork and place it on a serving dish. Use a slotted spoon to pile the vegetables around the pork. Thicken the liquid left in the slow cooker with guar or xanthan and serve the sauce with the pork and vegetables.

YIELD: 8 servings, each with: 396 calories, 23g fat, 36g protein, 11g carbohydrate, 1g dietary fibre, 10g usable carbs.

Onion–Mustard Pork Chops

1kg pork chops
1 tbsp (15ml) olive oil
1 medium onion, thinly sliced
4 cloves garlic, crushed
1 tsp dry mustard
1/2 tsp salt or Vege-Sal
1 tsp pepper
1 dash hot sauce
1 tbsp (15ml) cider vinegar
120ml dry white wine
2 tbsps (30g) brown mustard
120ml double cream
Guar or xanthan

In a big, heavy frying pan, brown the pork on both sides in the oil over medium-high heat. Transfer the pork to your slow cooker.

Turn the heat down to medium-low and add the onion to the frying pan. Sauté it until it's translucent. Then stir in the garlic, dry mustard, salt or Vege-Sal, pepper, and hot sauce and let the whole thing sauté for another minute or so. Transfer the mixture to the slow cooker on top of the pork.

In a bowl, stir together the vinegar and wine. Pour the mixture into the slow cooker. Cover the slow cooker, set it to low, and let it cook for 6 hours.

When the time's up, remove the pork to a serving dish. Stir the mustard and cream into the juice in the pot. Thicken the juice a tad with guar or xanthan and serve the sauce over the pork.

YIELD: 6 servings, each with: 352 calories, 25g fat, 25g protein, 4g carbohydrate, 1g dietary fibre, 3g usable carbs.

Choucroute Garni

This is a streamlined version of a traditional dish from the Alsace region of France. The name means Garnished Sauerkraut. It's so simple and very good, especially on a cold night.

    400g tinned sauerkraut, rinsed and drained
    1 tbsp (14ml) bacon grease
    60ml apple cider vinegar
    1 tbsp (1.5g) Splenda
    1/2 medium onion, thinly sliced
    2 tbsps (30ml) gin
    60ml dry white wine
    450g meat (Choose any combination of kielbasa, smoked sausage, frankfurters, link sausages, 5mm-thick ham slices, or smoked pork chops.*)

Place the sauerkraut in your slow cooker. Add the bacon grease, vinegar, Splenda, onion, gin, and wine and give it a quick stir. Place the meat on top. Cover the slow cooker, set it to low, and let it cook for 5 to 6 hours.

*I use 225g each of the lowest carbohydrate kielbasa and smoked sausage I can find.

> **NOTE:** This doesn't even start to fill my slow cooker, so feel free to double or even triple this recipe. If you increase it, I suggest arranging it with a layer of kraut, a layer of meat, a layer of kraut, and so on. And, of course, you'll have to increase the cooking time by an hour, maybe two, depending on how many extra layers you use.

YIELD: 3 servings, each with: 112 calories, 5g fat, 1g protein, 9g carbohydrate, 4g dietary fibre, 5g usable carbs. (This will depend on which meats you use.)

CHAPTER SIX

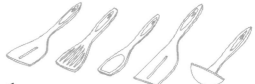

Slow Cooker Lamb

You'll notice a certain reliance on lamb shanks here. Lamb shanks are the bottom-most part of a leg of lamb, and they're ideal for slow cooking for a couple reasons. They fit neatly in the pot, and they're the sort of tough, flavourful meat that really shines with slow, moist cooking.

If you're having trouble finding lamb shanks at your supermarket, ask the nice meat blokes. Or you could make any of the shank recipes with a chunk of lamb leg or shoulder of the right weight. Have the meat guys cut it into a few pieces, though, so it'll fit in your pot and won't take far more cooking time than the recipe specifies. Most supermarkets will cut up a roast for you for no added charge.

Lamb Shanks in Red Wine

This is a hearty one-pot meal.

2.5kg lamb shank (4 shanks)
60ml olive oil
2 stalks celery, sliced 2cm thick
2 carrots, sliced 2cm thick
8 cloves garlic, crushed
1/2 onion, chunked
225g sliced mushrooms
235ml chicken stock
235ml dry red wine
1 tsp beef bouillon concentrate
2 tsps pepper
1/2 tsp ground rosemary
2 bay leaves
Guar or xanthan

In a big, heavy frying pan, sear the lamb all over in the oil.

Place the celery, carrots, garlic, onion, and mushrooms in your slow cooker.

When the lamb is browned all over, transfer it to the slow cooker, on top of
the veggies.

In a bowl, stir together the stock, wine, bouillon, pepper, and rosemary. Pour the
mixture over the lamb. Add the bay leaves. (Make sure they land in the liquid!)
Cover the slow cooker, turn it to low, and let it cook for 6 hours.

When the time's up, remove the lamb to serving plates. Using guar or xanthan, thicken
the liquid in the slow cooker to the consistency of double cream. Ladle the sauce and
vegetables over the lamb.

YIELD: 6 servings, each with: 757 calories, 50g fat, 59g protein, 8g carbohydrate,
2g dietary fibre, 6g usable carbs.

⌂ Lemon Lamb Shanks

Lemon brings out the best in lamb!

2kg lamb shank
2 tbsps (30ml) olive oil
1 tsp lemon pepper
$1/2$ tsp dry mustard
120ml chicken stock
1 tsp beef bouillon concentrate
$1/2$ tsp grated lemon peel
2 tbsps (30ml) lemon juice
1 tsp dried rosemary
2 cloves garlic, crushed
Guar or xanthan

Sear the lamb all over in the oil. Place the lamb in your slow cooker.

In a bowl, mix together the lemon pepper and dry mustard. Sprinkle the mixture evenly over the lamb.

In the same bowl, mix together the stock, bouillon, lemon peel, lemon juice, rosemary, and garlic. Pour the mixture over the lamb. Cover the slow cooker, set it to low, and let it cook for 8 hours.

When the time's up, remove the lamb and thicken up the liquid in the slow cooker a bit with guar or xanthan.

Serve this dish with a salad with plenty of cucumbers and tomatoes!

YIELD: 6 servings, each with: 535 calories, 37g fat, 46g protein, 1g carbohydrate, trace dietary fibre, 1g usable carbs.

Kashmiri Lamb Shanks

This was originally a recipe for a frying pan curry of lamb, but it works wonderfully in the slow cooker. If you like Indian food, you have to try this. And if you've never eaten Indian food, you need to start!

    1.25kg lamb shank
    2 tbsps (30ml) olive oil
    235ml chicken stock
    1/2 tsp beef bouillon concentrate
    1 tsp Garam Masala (see recipe page 236) or purchased garam masala
    2 tsps ground coriander
    1 tbsp (8g) grated ginger root
    1/4 tsp cayenne
    Guar or xanthan

In a big, heavy frying pan, sear the lamb all over in the oil over medium-high heat. Transfer the lamb to your slow cooker.

In a bowl, mix together the stock, bouillon, garam masala, coriander, ginger, and cayenne. Pour the mixture over the lamb. Cover the slow cooker, set it to low, and let it cook for 8 hours.

Remove the lamb to a serving dish, thicken the sauce a bit with guar or xanthan, and serve the sauce over the lamb.

YIELD: 4 servings, each with: 530 calories, 38g fat, 44g protein, 1g carbohydrate, trace dietary fibre, 1g usable carbs.

Seriously Simple Lamb Shanks

Simple is good!

> 1.5kg lamb shank
> 30ml olive oil
> 235ml chicken stock
> 1 tsp beef bouillon concentrate
> 2 tsps paprika
> 5 cloves garlic, crushed
> Guar or xanthan

Season the lamb all over with salt and pepper. In a big, heavy frying pan, over medium-high heat, sear the lamb in the oil until it's brown all over. Transfer the lamb to your slow cooker.

In a bowl, mix together the stock and bouillon. Pour the mixture over the lamb. Sprinkle the paprika and garlic over the lamb. Cover the slow cooker, set it to low, and let it cook for 6 to 7 hours.

Remove the lamb with tongs and put it on a serving plate. Pour the liquid in the slow cooker into a 500ml glass measuring jug and let the fat rise to the top. Skim the fat off and discard, and then thicken up the remaining liquid using guar or xanthan. Serve the sauce with the shanks.

Either Cauli-Rice (see recipe page 239) or Fauxtatoes (see recipe page 239) would be nice with this, but it's fine with just a simple salad or vegetable side.

YIELD: 4 servings, each with: 627 calories, 44g fat, 52g protein, 2g carbohydrate, trace dietary fibre, 2g usable carbs.

⊙ Lamb Stew Provençal

I turned this recipe over to my sister to test. She's nuts for French food, especially from Provence. She gave this the thumbs-up.

> 1.5kg lamb stew meat – shoulder is good, cubed.
> (Have the meat blokes cut it off the bone.)
> 3 tbsps (45ml) olive oil
> 1 whole fennel bulb, sliced lengthwise
> 1 medium onion, sliced lengthwise
> 4 cloves garlic, crushed
> 1 bay leaf
> 1 tsp dried rosemary, whole needles
> 425g tinned black soybeans, drained
> 235ml beef stock
> 1 tsp chicken bouillon concentrate
> 1/2 tsp dried basil
> 1/2 tsp dried marjoram
> 1/2 tsp dried savoury
> 1/2 tsp dried thyme
> Guar or xanthan

Season the lamb with salt and pepper. In a big, heavy frying pan, heat the oil and brown the lamb on all sides over medium-high heat.

Place the fennel, onion, and garlic in the bottom of your slow cooker. Add the bay leaf and rosemary. Dump the soybeans on top of that. When the lamb is browned, put it on top of the vegetables.

In a bowl, stir together the stock, bouillon, basil, marjoram, savoury, and thyme. Pour the mixture over the lamb. Cover the slow cooker, set it to low, and let it cook for 8 to 9 hours.

When it's done, thicken the liquid to the texture of double cream with guar or xanthan.

YIELD: 8 servings, each with: 348 calories, 17g fat, 41g protein, 8g carbohydrate, 4g dietary fibre, 4g usable carbs.

Caribbean Slow Cooker Lamb

Lamb and goat are very popular in the Caribbean, and this is my slow cooker interpretation of a Caribbean lamb dish. Look for tamarind concentrate in a supermarket with a good international section. I found it in a medium-size town in southern Indiana, so you may well find it near you! If you can't find it, you could use a tbsp of lemon juice and a tsp of Splenda instead. Your lamb will be less authentically Caribbean-tasting, but still yummy.

> 1–1.5kg of a leg of lamb
> 1/2 medium onion, chopped
> 1/2 tsp finely chopped garlic or 1 clove garlic, crushed
> 1 tsp tamarind concentrate
> 1 tbsp (15g) spicy brown mustard
> 260g tinned diced tomatoes
> 1 tsp hot sauce – preferably Caribbean Scotch Bonnet sauce
>   – more or less to taste
> Guar or xanthan (optional)

Place the lamb in your slow cooker.

In a bowl, stir together the onion, garlic, tamarind, mustard, tomatoes, and hot sauce. Pour the mixture over the lamb. Cover the slow cooker, set it to low, and let it cook for a good 8 hours.

When it's done, remove the lamb to a serving dish, thicken the pot juices with the guar or xanthan if it seems necessary, and add salt and pepper to taste.

YIELD: 6 servings, each with: 357 calories, 26g fat, 27g protein, 3g carbohydrate, 1g dietary fibre, 2g usable carbs.

CHAPTER SEVEN

Slow Cooker
Fish and Seafood

I don't generally think of fish when I think of long, slow cooking, and indeed who wants to leave fish in a slow cooker all day? But the gentle, even heating of your slow cooker, used judiciously, can yield fish and seafood that's remarkably moist and tender. When you don't need to have dinner waiting, try these recipes!

Or, as in a few of these recipes, you can cook everything else all day, and then just stir in the seafood for the last little bit of cooking time. It doesn't take long to cook fish or seafood through!

Lime-Basted Scallops

My seafood-loving husband thought these were some of the best scallops he'd ever had.

  60ml lime juice
  45g butter
  2 cloves garlic
  680g scallops
  Guar or xanthan
  5g chopped fresh coriander

Put the lime juice, butter, and garlic in your slow cooker. Cover the slow cooker, set it to high, and let it cook for 30 minutes.

Uncover the slow cooker and stir the butter, lime juice, and garlic together. Now add the scallops, stirring them around to coat them with the sauce. Spread them in a single layer on the bottom of the slow cooker. (If the sauce seems to pool in one or two areas, try to cluster the scallops there. In my pot, the sauce liked to stay around the edges.) Re-cover the pot, set it to high, and let it cook for 45 minutes.

When the time's up, remove the scallops to serving plates. Thicken the pot liquid just a tiny bit with guar or xanthan and spoon the sauce over the scallops. Top each serving with a tbsp of coriander.

YIELD: 4 servings, each with: 233 calories, 10g fat, 29g protein, 6g carbohydrate, trace dietary fibre, 6g usable carbs.

⛾ Lemon-Mustard Salmon Steaks

This is so simple and classic. The salmon comes out tender and moist.

> 30g butter
> 1 tbsp (15ml) lemon juice
> 1 tsp Dijon mustard
> 1 pinch salt or Vege-Sal
> 2 salmon steaks, totaling about 450g
> 2 tbsps (8g) chopped fresh parsley

Combine the butter, lemon juice, mustard, and salt or Vege-Sal in your slow cooker. Cover the slow cooker, set it to low, and let it cook for 30 to 40 minutes. Stir together.

Now put the salmon steaks in the slow cooker and turn them once or twice to coat. Re-cover the slow cooker and let it cook for 1 hour. Spoon some of the pot liquid over the salmon and sprinkle with the parsley before serving.

2 servings, each with: 369 calories, 19g fat, 46g protein, 1g carbohydrate, trace dietary fibre, 1g usable carbs.

⛾ Maple-Balsamic Salmon

This started as a recipe for grilled salmon in *The Low-Carb Barbeque Book*, but it works brilliantly in the slow cooker, as well.

> 2 salmon steaks, totaling about 450g
> 1 tbsp (15ml) olive oil
> 60g sugar-free pancake syrup
> 1 clove garlic, crushed
> 1 tbsp (14ml balsamic vinegar)

In your slow cooker, combine everything but the salmon. Cover the slow cooker, set it to low, and let it cook for 30 minutes.

Now add the salmon, turning the steaks to coat them with the sauce. Re-cover the pot and let it cook for 1 hour. Spoon some of the pot liquid over the steaks before serving.

YIELD: 2 servings, each with: 326 calories, 15g fat, 45g protein, 1g carbohydrate, trace dietary fibre, 1g usable carbs.

Almond-Stuffed Flounder Rolls with Orange Butter Sauce

60g butter

2 tbsps (15ml) lemon juice

1/8 tsp orange extract

1 tsp Splenda

145g almonds

40g finely chopped onion

1 clove garlic, crushed

1 1/2 tsps Dijon mustard

1/2 tsp soy sauce

16g finely chopped fresh parsley, divided

450g flounder fillets, 115g each

Put half of the butter, the lemon juice, orange extract, and Splenda in your slow cooker. Cover the slow cooker, set it to low, and let it heat while you fix your flounder rolls.

Put the almonds in a food processor with the S-blade in place and grind them to a cornmeal consistency. Melt the other half of the butter in a medium-sized heavy frying pan and add the ground almonds. Stir the almonds over medium heat for 5 to 7 minutes, or until they smell toasty. Transfer them to a bowl.

Now melt the final tbsp of butter in the frying pan and sauté the onion and garlic over medium-low heat until the onion is just turning translucent. Add them to the almonds and stir them in. Now stir in the mustard, soy sauce, and most of the parsley.

Lay the flounder fillets on a big plate and divide the almond mixture between them. Spread it over the fillets, and then roll each one up and fasten it with a toothpick.

Take the lid off the slow cooker and stir the sauce. Place the flounder rolls in the sauce and spoon the sauce over them. Re-cover the pot and let the rolls cook for 1 hour. When they're done, spoon the sauce over the rolls and sprinkle the remaining parsley over them to serve.

YIELD: 4 servings, each with: 285 calories, 19g fat, 24g protein, 5g carbohydrate, 2g dietary fibre, 3g usable carbs.

⊡ Sweet and Sour Shrimp

Adding the shrimp and mange tout at the last moment keeps them from becoming desperately overcooked.

 peaches, peeled and cubed (Frozen unsweetened peaches work well. Just cut them into smaller 2cm chunks)
 50g chopped onion
 1 green bell pepper, diced
 60g chopped celery
 120ml chicken stock
 30ml dark sesame oil
 60ml soy sauce
 30ml rice vinegar
 60ml lemon juice
 1 tsp red pepper flakes
 1 tbsp (1.5g) Splenda
 170g fresh mange tout, trimmed
 700g shrimp, shells removed
 100g slivered almonds, toasted
 Guar or xanthan

Put the peaches, onion, pepper, celery, stock, sesame oil, soy sauce, vinegar, lemon juice, red pepper flakes, and Splenda in your slow cooker and stir them together. Cover the slow cooker, set it to low, and let it cook for 4 hours. (Or you could cook it on high for 2 hours.)

When the time's up, turn the pot up to high while you trim the mange tout and cut them in 2cm lengths. Stir them in and let it cook for 15 to 20 minutes. Now stir in the shrimp. If they're uncooked, give them 10 minutes, or until they're pink through. If they're cooked already, just give them 5 minutes or so, to get hot through.

You can serve this over rice for the carb-eaters in the family, of course. If you like, you can have yours on Cauli-Rice (see recipe page 239), but this dish is high-carb enough already that I'd probably eat it plain.

YIELD: 6 servings, each with: 257 calories, 11g fat, 27g protein, 13g carbohydrate, 3g dietary fibre, 10g usable carbs.

⊕ Pantry Seafood Supper

This is convenient because, as the name strongly suggests, it uses seafood you've got sitting in your pantry. If, instead, you've got seafood sitting in your freezer, you can use it instead – just let it cook an extra 30 minutes or so to make sure it's thawed and cooked through.

35g roasted red peppers jarred in oil, diced small
   (about 1 pepper)
20g chopped parsley
100g chopped mushrooms
175ml chicken stock
175ml dry white wine
2 tbsps (20g) finely chopped onion
2 tsps dried dill weed
1/2 tsp paprika
1/2 tsp Tabasco sauce
1 cup semi-skimmed milk
60ml double cream
Guar or xanthan
170g tinned tuna, drained
170g tinned crab, drained
170g tinned shrimp, drained

Combine the red peppers, parsley, mushrooms, stock, wine, onion, dill, paprika, and Tabasco sauce in your slow cooker. Cover the slow cooker, set it to low, and let it cook for 3 to 4 hours.

When the time's up, stir in the milk and cream and thicken the sauce to your liking with guar or xanthan. Now stir in the tuna, crab, and shrimp and let it cook for another 15 to 20 minutes.

Now you have a choice: You can eat this as a chowder, or you can serve it over Cauli-Rice (see recipe page 239) or low-carbohydrate pasta – or even over spaghetti squash. It's up to you.

YIELD: 4 servings, each with: 269 calories, 9g fat, 33g protein, 4g carbohydrate, 1g dietary fibre, 3g usable carbs.

CHAPTER EIGHT

Slow Cooker Crazy Mixed-Up Meals

It's really very hard to organize a cookbook. Take, for instance, the recipes that follow. They really messed up my plan to organize this book largely by protein source. After backing and forthing, moving them around, I threw up my hands and gave them their own chapter.

⊡ Simple Meat Loaf

This is simple, but it's hardly boring! Because meat loaf takes at least an hour in the oven, many of you may have given up on it as a weeknight dinner. Baking it in your slow cooker works remarkably well, although it doesn't brown much.

450g minced beef

450g pork sausage

1 medium onion, finely chopped

1 medium green pepper, finely chopped

25g oat bran

1/2 tsp pepper

1/2 tsp salt or Vege-Sal

30g Worcestershire sauce

2 eggs

60g pork rind crumbs (Run pork scratchings through your
food processor or blender.)

Place all ingredients in a big mixing bowl and use clean hands to smoosh everything together until it's well blended.

Put a rack or a collapsible basket-style steamer in the bottom of your slow cooker. Fold two squares of foil into strips and criss-cross them on the rack or steamer and up the sides of the slow cooker. (What you're doing is making a sling to help you lift the loaf out of the slow cooker.) If the holes/slots in your rack are pretty big, put a sheet of foil over the criss-crossed strips and pierce it all over with a fork.

Place the meat mixture on top of this and form into an evenly-domed meat loaf, smoothing the surface with dampened hands. Cover the slow cooker, set it to low, and let it cook for 9 to 12 hours.

Use the foil strips to lift the meat loaf out of the slow cooker.

YIELD: 8 servings, each with: 438 calories, 36g fat, 23g protein, 6g carbohydrate, 1g dietary fibre, 5g usable carbs.

Morty's Mixed Meat Loaf

The combination of meats makes this loaf unusually tasty.

2 rashers of cooked bacon, crumbled

450g minced beef

450g minced pork

450g minced turkey

3 stalks celery, finely chopped

30g finely chopped fresh parsley

120g Dana's No-Sugar Ketchup (see recipe page 228)
    or purchased low-carb ketchup

1 tsp hot sauce

2 eggs

60g barbeque-style pork rind crumbs
    (Just run 'em through your food processor.)

2 tbsps (30ml) Worcestershire sauce

1 tsp lemon juice

1/2 tsp dried marjoram

1 tsp salt or Vege-Sal

1/2 tsp pepper

Put a rack or basket-style steamer in the bottom of your slow cooker pot. Fold two squares of foil into strips and criss-cross them on the rack or steamer and up the sides of the slow cooker. (What you're doing is making a sling to help you lift the loaf out of the slow cooker.) If the holes/slots in your rack are pretty big, put a sheet of foil over the criss-crossed strips and pierce it all over with a fork.

Place all your ingredients in a big bowl and, using clean hands, smoosh everything together really well. Form it into a round loaf on the rack in the slow cooker. Cover the slow cooker, set it to low, and let it cook for 8 to 10 hours.

Use the strips of foil to lift the loaf out of the slow cooker.

YIELD: 8 servings, each with: 453 calories, 30g fat, 37g protein, 7g carbohydrate, 2g dietary fibre, 5g usable carbs.

☐ Pizza Stew

Here's a slow cooker meal for your pizza-craving family. Maria gets the credit for perfecting this one. It wasn't quite right the way I originally conceived it. Maria gave me feedback, we went with her suggestions, and success was ours!

450g Italian sausage meat
450g minced beef
1 green bell pepper, diced
25g diced onion
425ml no-sugar-added pizza sauce (Ragu makes one.)
220g shredded mozzarella cheese
40g shredded Parmesan cheese

In a big, heavy frying pan, brown and crumble the sausage and beef together. Drain them well and transfer them to your slow cooker. Add the pepper and onion and stir. Stir in the pizza sauce. Cover the slow cooker, set it to low, and let it cook for 5 to 6 hours.

Now uncover the slow cooker and top the stew with the mozzarella cheese. Re-cover the slow cooker and let it cook for another 30 to 45 minutes, to melt the cheese. Serve with the Parmesan cheese sprinkled on top.

YIELD: 6 servings, each with: 626 calories, 49g fat, 37g protein, 8g carbohydrate, 2g dietary fibre, 6g usable carbs.

⌷ Low-Carb Slow Cooker Paella

Maria, who tested this, rates it a 10. She added, 'While this won't fool a purist, the flavour is quite good. For those who can't afford saffron, turmeric is an acceptable substitute. For an authentic presentation, which is important, put the 'rice' in a paella pan or flat casserole, mix it with the veggies, and arrange the chicken and shrimp artistically on top.' Do look for Spanish chorizo, rather than Mexican chorizo, for this dish.

6 chicken leg and side quarters, about 1.5kg

60ml olive oil

130g chopped onion

1 clove garlic, crushed

1 green bell pepper

170g chorizo sausages or diced ham

410g tinned tomatoes, drained

1/2 tsp saffron threads

235ml chicken stock

1 tsp chicken bouillon concentrate

170g shrimp

40g fresh mange tout, cut into 2cm pieces

1 head cauliflower

In a big, heavy frying pan, brown the chicken in the oil.

While that's happening, put the onion, garlic, and green pepper in your slow cooker. When the chicken is brown, transfer it to the slow cooker as well.

If using chorizo, slice it into rounds and brown it in the same frying pan, then transfer it to the slow cooker. If using ham, you can simply add it directly to the slow cooker. Place the tomatoes on top of that.

In a bowl, mix together the saffron, stock, and bouillon and pour it into the slow cooker. Cover the slow cooker, set it to low, and let it cook for 6 hours.

When the time's up, turn the slow cooker to high. Add the shrimp and mange tout to the slow cooker, re-cover, and cook for another 30 minutes.

While that's happening, shred the cauliflower in your food processor, put it in a microwavable casserole dish with a lid, add a few tbsps of water, cover, and microwave it on high for 8 to 9 minutes. Serve with the paella.

YIELD: 8 servings, each with: 599 calories, 42g fat, 46g protein, 8g carbohydrate, 1g dietary fibre, 7g usable carbs.

☺ Albondigas en Salsa Chipotle

Mexican meatballs! Yummy.

1/2 medium onion, chopped

1 tbsp (15ml) oil

1 tsp ground cumin

1 tsp ground coriander

3 cloves garlic, crushed

1 tsp dried oregano

1 tsp dried thyme

410g tinned tomatoes with green chillies, drained

235ml chicken stock

1/2 tsp chicken bouillon concentrate

1 chipotle chile tinned in adobo sauce, or more to taste

450g minced beef

455g ground turkey

1 egg

1 tsp pepper

1/2 tsp ground allspice

1/2 tsp ground cumin

1/2 tsp ground coriander

1 tsp dried oregano

2 tsps salt or Vege-Sal

1/2 medium onion, finely chopped

3 cloves garlic, crushed

30ml olive oil

1 tsp guar or xanthan

In a big, heavy frying pan, sauté 1/2 onion in the 1 tbsp oil over medium-high heat until translucent. Add the 1 tsp ground cumin, 1 tsp ground coriander, 3 cloves garlic, 1 tsp oregano, and 1 tsp thyme and sauté for another minute or two. Transfer the mixture to your blender or food processor.

Add the tomatoes, stock, bouillon, and chipotle. Blend until smooth and pour into your slow cooker. Cover the slow cooker, set it to low, and start it cooking as you make the meatballs.

Place the beef, turkey, egg, pepper, allspice, 1/2 tsp ground cumin, 1/2 tsp ground coriander, 1 tsp oregano, salt or Vege-Sal, 1/2 onion, and 3 cloves garlic into a big bowl and use clean hands to smoosh it all together. Form it into meatballs.

In the frying pan, heat 2 tbsps oil over medium-high heat and brown the meatballs on all sides. Transfer the meatballs to the slow cooker, re-cover, and let the whole thing cook for 3 to 4 hours.

Scoop the meatballs out with a slotted spoon and put them in a serving bowl. Thicken the sauce to taste with the guar or xanthan and pour the sauce over the meatballs.

YIELD: 8 servings, each with: 297 calories, 20g fat, 23g protein, 5g carbohydrate, 1g dietary fibre, 4g usable carbs.

Brunswick Stew

This is an old favourite, de-carbed and updated for your slow cooker.

> 1 large onion, sliced
> 1kg skinless chicken thighs
> 210g ham cubes, cooked
> 1 tsp dry mustard
> 1 tsp dried thyme
> 1/2 tsp pepper
> 260g tinned diced tomatoes
> 400g chicken stock
> 3 cloves garlic, crushed
> 1 tbsp (15g) Worcestershire sauce
> 1/4 tsp hot sauce, or to taste
> 170g tinned black soybeans, drained

Place the onion in your slow cooker first. Add the chicken and ham.

In a bowl, mix together the dry mustard, thyme, pepper, tomatoes, stock, garlic, Worcestershire sauce, and hot sauce. Pour the mixture over the chicken and ham. Cover the slow cooker, set it to low, and let it cook for 8 hours.

When the time's up, stir in the soybeans and let the whole thing cook for another 20 minutes or so.

YIELD: 6 servings, each with: 212 calories, 10g fat, 21g protein, 9g carbohydrate, 3g dietary fibre, 6g usable carbs.

CHAPTER NINE

Slow Cooker Soups

If there's a type of dish for which the slow cooker seems custom-made, it's soups. How wonderful to come home tired on a cold evening to a pot of hot, hearty, homemade soup!

Black Bean Soup

One of the few carb-y dishes I sometimes miss is legume soup, especially black bean soup. This is my de-carbed version.

> 800g tinned black soybeans
>
> 400g tinned black beans
>
> 475ml chicken stock
>
> 1 medium onion, cut into chunks
>
> 4 cloves garlic, crushed
>
> 1 medium carrot, shredded
>
> 2 medium stalks celery, finely diced
>
> 1 tsp salt or Vege-Sal
>
> 1/2 tsp pepper
>
> 1 tbsp (15ml) liquid smoke flavouring
>
> (for this specialist ingredient, try www.uniqueingredients.co.uk)
>
> 2 tsps hot sauce
>
> 230g ham cubes

Using your food processor with the S-blade in place, puree the soybeans and black beans. Place them in your slow cooker. Stir in the stock.

Place the onion in the food processor. Add the garlic, carrot, and celery. Pulse the food processor until everything is finely chopped. Add to the soup.

Stir in the salt or Vege-Sal, pepper, liquid smoke flavouring, hot sauce, and ham. Cover the slow cooker, set it to low, and let it cook for 9 to 10 hours.

When the time's up, stir the soup up (it'll have settled out some) and check to see if it needs more salt and pepper. (This will depend on how salty your ham is.)

YIELD: 8 servings, each with: 218 calories, 9g fat, 19g protein, 17g carbohydrate, 9g dietary fibre, 8g usable carbs.

⬚ Bollito Misto

All this Italian soup-stew needs with it is a green salad, and maybe some crusty bread for the carb-eaters.

    1 large onion, sliced
    2 carrots, cut 2cm thick
    3 stalks celery, cut 2cm thick
    1kg beef stewing steak, cubed
    1/2 tsp salt
    1/2 tsp pepper
    2 tbsps (8g) chopped fresh parsley
    1 bay leaf
    3 tsps chicken bouillon concentrate
    1 litre chicken stock
    1kg boneless, skinless chicken thighs, cubed
    450g Italian sausage links
    130g purchased pesto sauce

Put the onion, carrots, and celery in your slow cooker. Season the beef with the salt and pepper and place them on top. Add the parsley and bay leaf. Stir the bouillon into the chicken and pour it into the slow cooker. Cover the slow cooker, set it to low, and let it cook for 5 to 6 hours.

Add the chicken, turn the heat up to high, and let the whole thing cook another hour.

While it's cooking, pour yourself a glass of Chianti, and put out some vegetables and dip for the kids. In a big, heavy frying pan, place the sausages, cover with water, slap a lid on, and simmer for 20 minutes over medium heat. Remove the frying pan from the heat and leave the sausages in the water, with the lid on.

When the slow cooker's time is up, drain the sausage and cut it into 3cm chunks. Stir the sausage into the stuff in the slow cooker. Now ladle the whole thing into soup bowls and top each serving with a tbsp of pesto.

YIELD: 8 servings, each with: 599 calories, 43g fat, 44g protein, 6g carbohydrate, 1g dietary fibre, 5g usable carbs.

⟨∴⟩ Cauliflower, Cheese, and Spinach Soup

Maria's family gave this rave reviews. It's easy, too!

900g cauliflower florets, cut into 2cm pieces

1 litre chicken stock

80g finely chopped red onion

140g bagged baby spinach leaves, pre-washed

1/4 tsp cayenne

1/2 tsp salt or Vege-Sal

1/4 tsp pepper

4 cloves garlic, crushed

675g grated smoked Gouda cheese

235ml semi-skimmed milk

Guar or xanthan

In your slow cooker, combine the cauliflower, stock, onion, spinach, cayenne, salt or Vege-Sal, pepper, and garlic. Cover the slow cooker, set it to low, and let it cook for 6 hours, or until the cauliflower is tender.

When the time's up, stir in the Gouda, a little at a time, and then the milk. Re-cover the slow cooker and cook for another 15 minutes, or until the cheese has thoroughly melted. Thicken soup a little with guar or xanthan.

YIELD: 8 servings, each with: 214 calories, 14g fat, 17g protein, 7g carbohydrate, 2g dietary fibre, 5g usable carbs.

Cream of UnPotato Soup

I never cease to marvel at the versatility of cauliflower. This really does taste like potato soup.

> 1 litre chicken stock
> 1/2 head cauliflower, chunked
> 50g chopped onion
> 50g Ketatoes mix
> 120ml double cream
> 120ml semi-skimmed milk
> Guar or xanthan (optional)
> 5 spring onions, sliced

Put the stock, cauliflower, and onion in your slow cooker. Cover the slow cooker, set it to low, and let it cook for 4 to 5 hours.

I use a hand blender to puree my soup right in the slow cooker, but you may transfer the cauliflower and onion, along with a cup of stock, into your blender or food processor instead. Either way, puree until completely smooth, then blend in the Ketatoes. If you have removed the cauliflower from the slow cooker to puree, pour the puree back in, and whisk it into the remaining stock.

Stir in the cream and milk. Thicken it a bit further with guar or xanthan if you feel it needs it. Add salt and pepper to taste and stir in the sliced spring onions. Serve hot right away or chill and serve as vichyssoise.

YIELD: 6 servings, each with: 190 calories, 11g fat, 12g protein, 13g carbohydrate, 6g dietary fibre, 7g usable carbs.

German UnPotato Soup

This is worth the time you spend cutting things up! It's hearty and filling.

        1 head cauliflower, chunked
        2 stalks celery, sliced
        1 medium onion, chopped
        225g smoked sausage, sliced
        1 tbsp (30ml) oil
        1 litre beef stock
        2 tbsps (30ml) vinegar
        1 tbsp (1.5g) Splenda
        1/4 tsp celery seed
        1/2 tsp dry mustard
        1/4 tsp pepper
        240g bagged coleslaw mix

Place the cauliflower, celery, and onion in your slow cooker.

In a big, heavy frying pan, brown the sausage a bit in the oil. Transfer the sausage to the slow cooker, too.

Pour a quarter of the stock into the frying pan and stir it around a bit to dissolve the flavourful bits. Pour it into the slow cooker.

In a bowl, combine the rest of the stock with the vinegar, Splenda, celery seed, dry mustard, and pepper. Pour over the vegetables and sausage. Cover the slow cooker, set it to low, and let it cook for 8 hours.

When the time's up, stir in the coleslaw mix and let it cook for another 20 to 30 minutes.

YIELD: 4 servings, each with: 344 calories, 22g fat, 20g protein, 17g carbohydrate, 2g dietary fibre, 15g usable carbs.

Maria's New England Clam Chowder

This one is from my tester and dear friend Maria. She says, 'This was so good that I called my brother Peter over and made him try it. He was very impressed. He's a big clam chowder fan, and he said that our grandmother would approve.'

4 rashers of bacon, diced
1 medium onion, chopped
1 large turnip, cut in 2cm cubes
450g tinned clams, undrained
3 cloves garlic, crushed
1 tsp salt
1/2 tsp pepper
475ml double cream
30g butter

In a big, heavy frying pan, sauté the bacon, onion, and turnip until the onion is golden. Drain and put it on the bottom of your slow cooker.

Pour the clam liquid into a half-litre measuring jug and add enough water to make 500ml. In a bowl, combine the liquid and water mixture, the clams, garlic, salt, and pepper. Pour the mixture into the slow cooker. Cover the slow cooker, set it to low, and let it cook for 5 hours, or until the turnips are tender. Blend in the cream and butter during the last 45 minutes of cooking.

YIELD: 5 servings, each with: 550 calories, 44g fat, 27g protein, 11g carbohydrate, 1g dietary fibre, 10g usable carbs.

◌ Cream of Mushroom Soup

If you've only ever thought of mushroom soup as gooey stuff that came in tins and was used in casseroles, you need to try this! It has a rich, earthy flavour. Even my mushroom-phobic husband liked it.

225g mushrooms, sliced
25g chopped onion
2 tbsps (30g) butter
1 litre chicken stock
120ml double cream
120g light sour cream
Guar or xanthan (optional)

In a big, heavy frying pan, sauté the mushrooms and onion in the butter until the mushrooms soften and change colour. Transfer them to your slow cooker. Add the stock. Cover the slow cooker, set it to low, and let it cook for 5 to 6 hours.

When the time's up, scoop out the vegetables with a slotted spoon and put them in your blender or food processor. Add enough stock to help them process easily and puree them finely. Pour the pureed vegetables back into the slow cooker, scraping out every last bit with a rubber scraper. Now stir in the double cream and sour cream and add salt and pepper to taste. Thicken the sauce a bit with guar or xanthan if you think it needs it. Serve immediately.

YIELD: 5 servings, each with: 176 calories, 15g fat, 6g protein, 5g carbohydrate, 1g dietary fibre, 4 usable carbs.

Chicken and Vegetable Soup with Thai Spices

This soup is light, fragrant, and wonderful.

2 tbsps (30ml) oil

2 carrots, thinly sliced

4 stalks celery, thinly sliced

200g sliced mushrooms

1/2 medium onion, thinly sliced

2 cloves garlic, crushed

700g boneless, skinless chicken breast, cut into 2cm cubes

2 litres chicken stock

300g frozen cross-cut green beans

1 tbsp (8g) grated ginger root

9 tsps chilli paste

1 tbsp (15ml) lemon juice

1 tbsp (15ml) lime juice

1/8 tsp anise seed, ground

1/4 tsp ground cardamom

1/4 tsp ground cinnamon

1/2 tsp ground cumin

1/4 tsp ground coriander

1 tbsp (18g) fish sauce

Fresh coriander

Heat the oil in a big, heavy frying pan over medium-high heat and sauté the carrots, celery, mushrooms, and onion until the onion is starting to get translucent. Transfer them to your slow cooker, adding the garlic. Now add the chicken to the frying pan and sauté just until it's sealed on the outside. Transfer it to the slow cooker, too.

Pour in the stock and add the green beans, ginger, chilli paste, lemon juice, lime juice, anise seed, cardamom, cinnamon, cumin, coriander, and fish sauce. Stir, cover the slow cooker, set it to low, and let it cook for 6 to 8 hours.

Scatter a little coriander over each bowlful before serving.

YIELD: 8 servings, each with: 209 calories, 8g fat, 25g protein, 9g carbohydrate, 2g dietary fibre, 7g usable carbs.

⊙ Chicken Soup with Wild Rice

Wild rice has more fibre, and therefore fewer usable carbs, than regular rice, either white or brown. And it adds a certain cachet to your soup!

2 litres chicken stock
2 carrots, thinly sliced
2 stalks celery, diced
50g chopped onion
450g boneless, skinless chicken breast, cut into 2cm cubes
40g wild rice
1 tsp poultry seasoning

Simply combine everything in your slow cooker, cover, set it to low, and let it cook for 6 to 7 hours.

YIELD: 6 servings, each with: 182 calories, 4g fat, 25g protein, 10g carbohydrate, 2g dietary fibre, 8g usable carbs.

Mexican Beef and Bean Soup

You know the family will love this!

340g minced beef

1 medium onion, chopped

2 cloves garlic, crushed

1 medium green bell pepper, diced

1 litre beef stock

1 tsp beef bouillon concentrate

410g tinned tomatoes with green chillies

425g tinned black soybeans

2 tsps ground coriander

1 tsp ground cumin

4 tbsps (16g) chopped coriander

70g sour cream

In a big, heavy frying pan, brown and crumble the beef mince. Drain it well and transfer it to your slow cooker.

Add the onion, garlic, bell pepper, stock, bouillon, tomatoes, soybeans, coriander, and cumin and stir. Cover the slow cooker, set it to low, and let it cook for 7 to 8 hours.

Top each bowlful with coriander and sour cream.

YIELD: 6 servings, each with: 296 calories, 16g fat, 25g protein, 14g carbohydrate, 5g dietary fibre, 9g usable carbs.

⊙ Chicken Minestrone

Here's a de-carbed version of the Italian favourite. You'll never miss the pasta!

    3 rashers of bacon, chopped
    1 medium onion, chopped
    2 medium turnips, cut into 2cm cubes
    1 medium carrot, thinly sliced
    2 small courgette, quartered and sliced
    2 stalks celery, thinly sliced
    3 tbsps (45ml) olive oil
    1.5 litres chicken stock
    700g skinless chicken thighs, boned and cubed
    1 tbsp (4g) Italian seasoning
    410g tinned diced tomatoes, undrained
    425g tinned black soybeans

Spray a big, heavy frying pan with nonstick cooking spray, then start the bacon frying over medium heat. As some grease cooks out of the bacon, add as many of the vegetables as will fit and sauté them until they soften just a bit. Transfer the vegetables to your slow cooker and continue sautéing the rest of the vegetables, adding oil as needed, until all the vegetables are softened a bit, and in the slow cooker.

Place the stock, chicken, Italian seasoning, tomatoes, soybeans, and salt and pepper to taste in the slow cooker. Cover the slow cooker, set it to low, and let it cook for 7 to 8 hours.

YIELD: 6 servings, each with: 294 calories, 16g fat, 21g protein, 18g carbohydrate, 6g dietary fibre, 12g usable carbs.

Spicy Chicken and Mushroom Soup

This is exotic and delicious.

45g butter

1 leek, thinly sliced (white part only)

225g sliced mushrooms

1 clove garlic, crushed

2 tsps Garam Masala (see recipe page 236) or purchased garam masala

1 tsp pepper

1/4 tsp cayenne

1/4 tsp ground nutmeg

1 litre chicken stock

340g boneless, skinless chicken breasts, cut into thin strips

120ml semi-skimmed milk

120ml double cream

3 tbsps (12g) chopped fresh coriander (optional)

Melt the butter in a big, heavy frying pan, over medium heat, and sauté the leek with the mushrooms until they both soften. Stir in the garlic, Garam Masala, pepper, cayenne, and nutmeg and sauté for another minute or two. Transfer to your slow cooker. Pour in the stock and add the chicken. Cover the slow cooker, set it to low, and let it cook for 6 to 7 hours.

When the time's up, use a slotted spoon to scoop roughly two-thirds of the solids into your blender or food processor. Add a cup or so of the stock and puree until smooth. Stir the puree back into the rest of the soup. (You may want to rinse the blender or food processor out with a little stock, to get all of the puree.) Stir in the Carb Countdown and cream. Re-cover the pot and let it cook for another 30 minutes. Serve with coriander on top. Or not, if you prefer, it's nice without it, too!

YIELD: 6 servings, each with: 243 calories, 16g fat, 18g protein, 6g carbohydrate, 1g dietary fibre, 5g usable carbs.

☕ Tavern Soup

Cheese soup with beer! Don't worry about the kids, the alcohol cooks off.

 1 1/2 litres chicken stock
 30g finely diced celery
 30g finely diced green bell pepper
 30g shredded carrot
 16g chopped fresh parsley
 1/2 tsp pepper
 450g strong cheddar cheese, shredded
 350ml light beer
 1/2 tsp salt or Vege-Sal
 1/4 tsp Tabasco sauce
 Guar or xanthan

Combine the stock, celery, green pepper, carrot, parsley, and pepper in your slow cooker. Cover the slow cooker, set it to low, and let it cook for 6 to 8 hours, and even a bit longer won't hurt.

When the time's up, either use a hand-held blender to puree the vegetables right there in the slow cooker or scoop them out with a slotted spoon, puree them in your blender, and return them to the slow cooker.

Now whisk in the cheese a little at a time, until it's all melted in. Add the beer, salt or Vege-Sal, and Tabasco sauce and stir till the foaming stops. Use guar or xanthan to thicken your soup until it's about the texture of double cream. Re-cover the pot, turn it to high, and let it cook for another 20 minutes before serving.

YIELD: 8 servings, each with: 274 calories, 20g fat, 18g protein, 3g carbohydrate, trace dietary fibre, 3g usable carbs.

Turkey Sausage Soup

This is a great, filling family soup for a cold night.

- 700g bulk turkey sausage
- 410g tinned chopped tomatoes
- 225g tinned, sliced mushrooms
- 1 turnip, diced
- 150g cauliflower, diced
- 50g chopped onion
- 120g chopped green bell pepper
- 1 litre chicken stock
- 2 tsps chicken bouillon concentrate
- 1 tsp dried basil
- 2 tsps prepared horseradish
- 235ml double cream

In a large, heavy frying pan, brown and crumble the sausage. Pour off the fat and put the sausage in your slow cooker. Add the tomatoes, mushrooms, turnip, cauliflower, onion, and green pepper.

In a bowl, stir the stock and bouillon together. Stir in the basil and horseradish. Pour the mixture into the slow cooker. Cover the slow cooker, set it to low, and let it cook for 7 to 8 hours.

When the time's up, stir in the cream and let it cook for another 10 to 15 minutes.

YIELD: 6 servings, each with: 666 calories, 61g fat, 17g protein, 12g carbohydrate, 2g dietary fibre, 10g usable carbs.

⊙ Seafood Chowder

My sister Kim, who tested this for me, said that you don't have to stick to shrimp. You could use crab, chunks of lobster tail, or even a cut-up firm-fleshed fish fillet. Don't use fake seafood – 'delicacies' and such. It has a lot of added carbs.

225g shredded cauliflower

40g shredded carrots

1 tsp dried thyme

1 clove garlic

1 tbsp (10g) finely chopped green bell pepper

1/8 tsp cayenne

1/4 tsp pepper

700ml chicken stock

235ml semi-skimmed milk

60ml double cream

225g shrimp, shells removed

1 tbsp (5g) Ketatoes mix

25g spring onions, thinly sliced

Guar or xanthan

Combine the cauliflower, carrots, thyme, garlic, green pepper, cayenne, pepper, and stock in your slow cooker. Cover the slow cooker, set it to low, and let it cook for 4 hours.

Turn the slow cooker to high and stir in the milk and cream. Re-cover the slow cooker and let it cook for another 30 to 45 minutes. If your shrimp are big, chop them coarsely during this time, but little, whole shrimp will look prettier, of course!

Stir in the Ketotoes mix. Now stir in the shrimp and re-cover the pot. If your shrimp are pre-cooked, just give them 5 minutes or so to heat through. If they're raw, give them 10 minutes. Stir in the spring onions and salt to taste. Thicken the stock with the guar or xanthan.

YIELD: 5 servings, each with: 164 calories, 8g fat, 17g protein, 7g carbohydrate, 2g dietary fibre, 5g usable carbs.

CHAPTER TEN

Slow Cooker Sides

My guess is you use your slow cooker mostly for main dishes, because that's the way it'll make your life the most convenient. Many of the main dishes in this book are complete meals, full of vegetables as well as protein, and they don't need a thing with them except a drink. With the main dishes that do need a side, the easiest and most appealing thing is often a salad.

Yet there are good reasons to cook a side dish in your slow cooker. Some of them just plain take less work and watching this way, like the Southern Beans. Sometimes you want to make an interesting side to go with a plain meat roasting in the oven and want to be able to ignore it for an hour or two or three while you do something else. In both of these instances, the slow cooker is your very good friend.

⛁ Barbeque Green Beans

These are fab!

> 600g cross-cut frozen green beans, unthawed
> 25g chopped onion
> 4 rashers of cooked bacon, drained and crumbled
> 75ml low-carb barbeque sauce
>   (see recipe page 231 or use purchased sauce)

Put the green beans in your slow cooker. Add the onion and bacon, then stir in the barbeque sauce. Cover the slow cooker, set it to high, and let it cook for 3 hours. (If you prefer, set it to low and let it cook for 5 to 6 hours.)

YIELD: 6 servings, each with: 58 calories, 2g fat, 3g protein, 8g carbohydrate, 2g dietary fibre, 6g usable carbs.

⛁ Southern Beans

American southerners will be shocked to know that I never tasted green beans slowly cooked with bacon until I moved to southern Indiana, but I liked them right away. Around our house, this recipe is jokingly referred to as The Sacred Masonic Vegetable, because my husband's never been to a Masonic banquet that didn't feature beans cooked this way!

> 600g frozen green beans, unthawed
> 35g diced onion
> 30g diced celery
> 4 rashers of bacon, cooked and crumbled
> 1 tbsp (18ml) bacon grease
> 120ml water

Place the beans in the slow cooker and stir in everything else. Cover the slow cooker, set it to low, and let it cook for 4 hours.

YIELD: 6 servings, each with: 75 calories, 4g fat, 3g protein, 7g carbohydrate, 3g dietary fibre, 4g usable carbs.

 Tangy Beans

600g frozen green beans, unthawed

25g chopped onion

30g chopped green bell pepper

60ml cider vinegar

2 tbsps (3g) Splenda

1/8 tsp black pepper

Combine everything in your slow cooker. Stir to distribute evenly. Cover the slow cooker, set it to low, and let it cook for 5 hours.

Serve with a pat of butter and a little salt.

YIELD: 4 servings, each with: 50 calories, trace fat, 2g protein, 12g carbohydrate, 4g dietary fibre, 8g usable carbs.

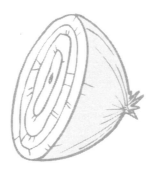

 Green Bean Casserole

800g frozen green beans, unthawed

100g chopped mushrooms

roasted red pepper, diced

25g chopped onion

2 tsps dried sage

1 tsp salt or Vege-Sal

1 tsp pepper

1/2 tsp ground nutmeg

235ml beef stock

1 tsp beef bouillon concentrate

120ml double cream

Guar or xanthan

100g slivered almonds

1 tbsp (15g) butter

Combine the green beans, mushrooms, red pepper, and onion in your slow cooker.

In a bowl, mix together the sage, salt or Vege-Sal, pepper, nutmeg, stock, and bouillon. Pour the mixture over the vegetables. Stir the whole thing up. Cover the slow cooker, set it to low, and let it cook for 5 to 6 hours.

When the time's up, stir in the cream and thicken the sauce a bit with guar or xanthan. Re-cover the slow cooker and let it stay hot while you sauté the almonds in the butter until golden. Stir them into the beans.

YIELD: 8 servings, each with: 191 calories, 14g fat, 7g protein, 12g carbohydrate, 4g dietary fibre, 8g usable carbs.

Basic Artichokes

2 artichokes

60ml lemon juice

Using kitchen shears, snip the pointy tips off the artichoke leaves. Split the artichokes down the middle, top to bottom, and scrape out the chokes.

Fill your slow cooker with water, add the lemon juice, and put in the artichokes. Cover the slow cooker, set it to high, and let it cook for 3 to 4 hours.

Drain the artichokes.

Serve the artichokes with the dipping sauce of your choice, such as lemon butter, mayonnaise, aioli, whatever you've got. If you have a big slow cooker, feel free to cook more artichokes!

YIELD: 2 servings, each with: 68 calories, trace fat, 4g protein, 16g carbohydrate, 7g dietary fibre, 9g usable carbs.

Maria's Slow Cooker Asparagus

Here's another recipe contributed by my pal and recipe tester Maria.

450g asparagus spears

1 tsp dried rosemary

1 clove garlic, crushed

1 tbsp (30ml) lemon juice

Snap off woody ends of the asparagus. Place trimmed asparagus on the bottom of your slow cooker. (If you're using a round cooker, you may need to cut them to fit.) Sprinkle the asparagus with the rosemary and garlic and pour the lemon juice on top. Cover the slow cooker, set it to low, and let it cook for 2 hours, or until the asparagus is tender.

YIELD: 4 servings, each with: 17 calories, trace fat, 1g protein, 4g carbohydrate, 1g dietary fibre, 3g usable carbs.

Spinach Parmesan Casserole

This is a lot like creamed spinach, only less — well, creamy.

570g frozen chopped spinach, thawed and drained*

75ml double cream

40g shredded Parmesan cheese

1 clove garlic, crushed

20g finely chopped onion

1 egg

1/2 tsp salt

Place all ingredients in a mixing bowl. Stir it to blend very well. Spray a 1 litre glass casserole dish with oil to prevent sticking. Put the spinach mixture in the casserole, smoothing the top.

Place the casserole dish in your slow cooker and carefully pour water around it up to 3cm off the rim. Cover the slow cooker, set it to low, and let it cook for 4 hours.

Uncover the slow cooker and turn it off at least 30 minutes before serving time, so the water cools enough that you can remove the dish without scalding yourself.

*Make sure your spinach is very well drained. It's best to put it in a colander and press it as hard as you can, turning it several times.

YIELD: 6 servings, each with: 109 calories, 8g fat, 7g protein, 5g carbohydrate, 3g dietary fibre, 2g usable carbs.

⊙ Macadangdang

Long-time readers know that I'm a big fan of Peg Bracken's cookbooks. This is my de-carbed version of Macadangdang Spinach Medley, which appeared in Peg's *I Hate To Cook Almanac*. It's named for her Aunt Henry Macadangdang, who married a Filipino gentleman of that name. I found the name so charming and euphonious, I thought I'd just call this version Macadangdang. My husband rates this a perfect 10, and I like it, too!

1/2 head cauliflower

280g frozen chopped spinach, thawed and drained

30g butter

25g chopped onion

1 clove garlic, crushed

4 eggs

120ml semi-skimmed milk

1 1/2 tsps salt or Vege-Sal

1/4 tsp pepper

40g grated Parmesan cheese

110g grated mozzarella cheese

Run the cauliflower through the shredding blade of your food processor. Place the resulting Cauli-Rice in a mixing bowl. Drain the thawed frozen spinach really well (I actually squeeze mine) and add it to the Cauli-Rice.

Melt the butter in a medium frying pan, over medium-low heat, and sauté the onion until it's just translucent. Add the garlic, sauté for another minute or two, then dump the whole thing in the bowl with the cauliflower and spinach.

Add the eggs, milk, salt or Vege-Sal, pepper, and Parmesan and stir the mixture / up quite well. Put it in a 1 1/2–2 litre casserole dish that you've sprayed with oil to prevent sticking. Cover the dish with foil and place it in your slow cooker. Pour water around it up to 3cm of the rim. Cover the slow cooker, set it to low, and let it cook for 2 1/2 hours.

Open the slow cooker and remove the foil. Sprinkle the mozzarella over your Macadangdang, put the foil back on, recover the pot, and let it cook for another 20 minutes, to melt the cheese. Then turn off the pot, uncover it, take off the foil, and let the whole thing cool just to the point where you can remove it from the water bath without scalding yourself, around 20 more minutes.

YIELD: 6 serving each with: 198 calories, 14g fat, 13g protein, 5g carbohydrate, 2g dietary fibre, 3g usable carbs.

⌂ Broccoli with Bacon and Pine Nuts

This is quite special. Don't cook your broccoli any longer than 2 hours!

450g frozen broccoli, unthawed

1 clove garlic, crushed

3 rashers of cooked bacon, crumbled

30g butter

1 tbsp (30ml) oil

30g pine nuts, toasted

Place the broccoli in your slow cooker. Stir in the garlic and crumble in the bacon. Cover the slow cooker, set it to low, and let it cook for 2 hours.

Before serving, stir in the butter and oil and top with the pine nuts.

YIELD: 3 servings, each with: 184 calories, 15g fat, 8g protein, 8g carbohydrate, 5g dietary fibre, 3g usable carbs.

Fauxtatoes

Fauxtatoes is the now nearly-universal name for cauliflower puree, used by low-carbers everywhere as a substitute for mashed potatoes. To make plain Fauxtatoes as a side dish to serve with a slow-cooked main dish, see recipe page 239. These are slow cooked Fauxtatoes with truly tasty additions.

Cheddar-Barbeque Fauxtatoes

My husband was crazy about these!

> 1/2 head cauliflower, cut into florets
> 120ml water
> 50g shredded cheddar cheese
> 2 tsps Classic Rub (see recipe page 234)
>   or purchased barbeque seasoning
> 2 tbsps (10g) Ketatoes mix

Put the cauliflower in your slow cooker, including the stem. Add the water. Cover the slow cooker, set it to high, and let it cook for 3 hours. (Or cook it on low for 5 to 6 hours.)

When the time's up, use a slotted spoon to scoop the cauliflower out of the slow cooker, into your blender or your food processor (have the S-blade in place) and puree it there, or you can drain off the water and use a hand-held blender to puree the cauliflower right in the pot. Either way, drain the cauliflower and puree it!

Stir in everything else, until the cheese has melted.

YIELD: 3 servings, each with: 120 calories, 7g fat, 8g protein, 6g carbohydrate, 3g dietary fibre, 3g usable carbs.

Italian Garlic and Herb Fauxtatoes

1/2 head cauliflower, cut into florets

120ml chicken stock

1 tsp Italian seasoning

1 clove garlic, crushed

30g cream cheese

Guar or xanthan

Place the cauliflower in your slow cooker. Add the stock, Italian seasoning, and garlic. Cover the slow cooker, set it to low, and let it cook for 5 to 6 hours. (Or cook it on high for 3 hours.)

When the time's up, either remove the cauliflower with a slotted spoon and put it in your blender or food processor (with the S-blade in place) and puree it, or drain the stock out of the slow cooker and use a hand-held blender to puree your cauliflower in the pot. Add the cream cheese and stir till melted.

The mixture will still be a little watery. Stir with a whisk as you use guar or xanthan to thicken it up a bit.

YIELD: 3 servings, each with: 46 calories, 4g fat, 2g protein, 2g carbohydrate, 1g dietary fibre, 1g usable carbs.

Ranch and Green Onion Fauxtatoes

This is great with anything with a barbeque flavour.

> 1 head cauliflower, cut into florets
> 235ml water
> 100g Ketatoes mix
> 6 tsps ranch-style dressing mix
> 4 spring onions, thinly sliced

Place the cauliflower in your slow cooker with the water. Cover the slow cooker, set it to low, and let it cook for 5 hours. (Or cook it on high for 3 hours.)

When the time's up, the easiest thing to do is use a hand blender to puree the cauliflower right in the slow cooker. Don't bother to drain the water first. Whisk in the Ketatoes, ranch dressing mix, and spring onions.

YIELD: 6 servings, each with: 170 calories, 3g fat, 14g protein, 23g carbohydrate, 11g dietary fibre, 12g usable carbs.

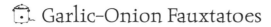 Garlic-Onion Fauxtatoes

Our tester Maria said her kids were particularly impressed by this!

> 1 head cauliflower, cut into florets
> 50g chopped onion
> 3 cloves garlic, crushed
> 150ml water
> 65g Ketatoes mix
> 45g butter

Place the cauliflower in your slow cooker. Add the onion, garlic, and water. Cover the slow cooker, set it to high, and let it cook for 2 1/2 to 3 hours. (Or cook it on low for 5 to 6 hours.)

When the time's up, use a hand-held blender to puree the cauliflower, onion, and garlic right there in the slow cooker. Alternatively, scoop it all into a food processor to puree, but you'll want the water in the pot, so if you transfer the vegetables, put the puree back in the pot with the water when you're done. Now stir in the Ketatoes, butter, and salt and pepper to taste.

YIELD: 6 servings, each with: 162 calories, 8g fat, 9g protein, 15g carbohydrate, 7g dietary fibre, 8g usable carbs.

Mashed Turnips

   2 large turnips, cubed
   25g chopped onion
   175ml beef stock

Put the turnips and onion in your slow cooker and add the stock. Cover the slow cooker, set it to low, and let it cook for 6 to 7 hours.

I like to mash these right in the pot with my hand-held blender, but if you prefer you can transfer them to your food processor or regular blender.

If you're going to serve these plain, you might add some butter, salt, and pepper, but if you're serving them with a gravy, they're great as is.

YIELD: 4 servings, each with: 31 calories, trace fat, 3g protein, 5g carbohydrate, 1g dietary fibre, 4g usable carbs.

Lemon–Parmesan Mushrooms

   225g mushrooms
   125ml chicken stock
   60ml lemon juice
   40g shredded Parmesan cheese
   16g chopped fresh parsley

Wipe the mushrooms clean with a damp cloth or paper towel, and put 'em in your slow cooker. Pour the stock and lemon juice over them. Cover the slow cooker, set it to low, and let it cook for 6 to 8 hours.

Remove the mushrooms from the slow cooker with a slotted spoon and put them on serving plates. Sprinkle with the Parmesan and parsley.

YIELD: 4 servings, each with: 65 calories, 3g fat, 6g protein, 5g carbohydrate, 1g dietary fibre, 4g usable carbs.

⌂ Baked Beans

This has a classic baked bean flavour and will be appreciated at any barbeque. I wouldn't attempt this recipe without a slow cooker. Do you have any idea how long it takes to cook soybeans soft? But with your slow cooker, you can just forget about them for 12 hours. If your health food store can't get you black soybeans (they're lower carb than white soybeans) you can order them online.

> 240g dry black soybeans
> 475ml water
> 50g chopped onion
> 1/2 tbsp (7ml) black treacle
> 3 tbsps (25g) low-carb ketchup (see recipe page 228)
> 1 tbsp dry mustard
> 2 tbsps (3g) Splenda
> 475ml water
> 340g smoked ham hocks

Put the soybeans in a big bowl and cover with the first 2 cups of water. Let them sit until the water is absorbed. Then put your soaked beans in the freezer overnight. (The freezing water will help break cell walls in the soybeans, making them soften faster when you cook them.)

When you want to cook the soybeans, thaw them, and pour off any soaking water. Put them in your slow cooker. Add the onion, treacle, ketchup, dry mustard, and Splenda. Pour the additional 2 cups of water over all and stir it up. Now dig a hole in the centre with a spoon, and plunk the ham hock down in it. Cover the slow cooker, set it to low, and let cook for 12 hours.

Fish out the ham hock with tongs, remove and discard the skin and bone. Chop the meat and stir it back into the beans before serving.

YIELD: 10 servings, each with: 286 calories, 15g fat, 8g protein, 12g carbohydrate, 11g dietary fibre, 1g usable carbs.

Bavarian Cabbage

This is great with the Sauerbrauten on page 89!

1 head red cabbage

1 medium onion, chopped

1 medium Granny Smith apple, chopped

6 rashers of cooked bacon, crumbled

2 tsps salt

235ml water

3 tbsps (4.5g) Splenda

150ml cider vinegar

3 tbsps (45ml) gin

Whack your head of cabbage in quarters, and remove the core. Then whack it into biggish chunks. Put it in a big mixing bowl. Add the onion, apple, and bacon to the cabbage. Toss everything together. Transfer the mixture to your slow cooker. (This will fill a 3-litre jobbie just about to overflowing! I barely got the top on mine.)

In a bowl, mix together the salt, water, Splenda, vinegar, and gin. Pour the mixture over the cabbage. Cover the slow cooker, set it to low, and let it cook for 6 to 8 hours.

YIELD: 6 servings, each with: 80 calories, 3g fat, 2g protein, 7g carbohydrate, 1g dietary fibre, 6g usable carbs.

⫱ Slow Cooker Chutney

This is the slow cooker version of my Major Gray's Chutney recipe from *500 More Low-Carb Recipes*. It's wonderful with anything curried.

> 1kg sliced peaches
> 30g ginger root slices
> 35g Splenda
> 3 cloves garlic
> 1 tsp red pepper flakes
> 1 tsp cloves
> 350ml cider vinegar
> Guar or xanthan

Combine everything but the guar or xanthan in your slow cooker. Cover the slow cooker, set it to low, and let it cook for 4 hours.

Take the lid off and let it cook for another hour, to let it cook down. Thicken a bit more, if you like, and store in an airtight container in the fridge.

YIELD: 32 servings (1 litre total), each with: 15 calories, trace fat, trace protein, 4g carbohydrate, 1g dietary fibre, 3g usable carbs.

⊡ Slow Cooker Cranberry Sauce

I like to have cranberry sauce on hand for those occasions when I don't want to do much cooking. It adds interest to plain roasted chicken (or even shop-bought rotisseried chicken.) It's easy to do, and makes plenty!

> 670g cranberries
> 235ml water
> 50g Splenda

Simply combine everything in your slow cooker and give it a stir. Cover the slow cooker, set it to low, and let it cook for 3 hours.

This won't be as syrupy as commercial cranberry sauce because of the lack of sugar. If this bothers you, you can thicken your sauce with your trusty guar or xanthan shaker, but I generally leave mine as is. This makes quite a lot, so divide it between three or four snap-top containers, and store it in the freezer. This way, you'll have cranberry sauce on hand whenever you bring home a rotisseried chicken!

YIELD: Makes about 22 servings of 2 tbsps, each with: 15 calories, trace fat, trace protein, 4g carbohydrate, 1g dietary fibre, 3g usable carbs.

⊙ Cranberry-Peach Chutney

This is seriously kicked-up from regular cranberry sauce! It's a natural with curried poultry, but try it with any simple poultry or pork dish.

340g cranberries
330g diced peaches
    (I use unsweetened frozen peach slices, diced.)
1 clove garlic, finely chopped
75mm ginger root, sliced into paper-thin rounds
1 lime, sliced paper-thin
30g Splenda
1 cinnamon stick
1 tsp mustard seed
1/4 tsp salt
1/4 tsp orange extract
1/4 tsp baking soda

Combine everything but the baking soda in your slow cooker. Cover the slow cooker, set it to low, and let it cook for 3 hours, stirring once halfway through.

When the time's up, stir in the baking soda and keep stirring till the fizzing subsides. Store in a tightly lidded container in the fridge. If you plan to keep it for long, freezing's a good idea.

Why baking soda? Because by neutralizing some of the acid in the cranberries, it lets you get away with less Splenda – and fewer carbs.

YIELD: Makes about 2 1/2 cups, or 20 servings of 2 tbsps, each with:
31 calories, trace fat, trace protein, 8g carbohydrate, 1g dietary fibre, 7g usable carbs.

CHAPTER ELEVEN

Slow Cooker Desserts

There are desserts that adapt well to the slow cooker, and then there are desserts that don't. In this chapter, I've really played to the slow cooker's strengths. Custards actually cook better in a slow cooker than in the oven, which is why you'll find half a dozen of them here. Indeed, they're so easy in the slow cooker, and so appealing and nutritious, you may find yourself making custard more often.

Your slow cooker also excels at baking cheesecake, though you may not know it yet. Give it a try!

Chocolate Fudge Custard

This really is dense and fudgy. It's intensely chocolatey, too.

        235ml semi-skimmed milk
        85g unsweetened baking chocolate
        16g Splenda
        235ml double cream
        1/2 tsp vanilla extract
        1 pinch salt
        6 eggs, beaten

In a saucepan, over the lowest possible heat (use a double boiler or heat diffuser if you have one) warm the Carb Countdown with the chocolate. When the chocolate melts, whisk the two together, then whisk in the Splenda.

Spray a 1.5 litre glass casserole dish with oil to prevent sticking. Pour the cream into it and add the chocolate mixture. Whisk in the vanilla extract and salt. Now add the eggs, one by one, whisking each in well before adding the next one.

Put the casserole dish in your slow cooker and pour water around it, up to 3cm of the top rim. Cover the slow cooker, set it to low, and let it cook for 4 hours.

Then turn off the slow cooker, remove the lid, and let the water cool enough so it won't scald you before removing the casserole dish. Chill the custard well before serving.

YIELD: 6 servings, each with: 299 calories, 28g fat, 10g protein, 6g carbohydrate, 2g dietary fibre, 4g usable carbs.

⌂ Flan

This is my slow cooker version of Maria's Flan from *500 Low-Carb Recipes*. Rich!

 2 tbsps (40g) sugar-free imitation honey
   (find this specialist ingredient online, try www.khwanabee.com)
 1 tsp black treacle
 235ml semi-skimmed milk
 235ml double cream
 6 eggs
 16g Splenda
 1 tsp vanilla
 1 pinch nutmeg
 1 pinch salt

Spray a 6-cup glass casserole dish with oil to prevent stickin. In a bowl, mix together the honey and the treacle. Pour the mixture into the bottom of the casserole dish.

In a mixing bowl, preferably one with a pouring lip, combine the milk, cream, eggs, Splenda, vanilla, nutmeg, and salt. Whisk everything together well. Pour the mixture into the casserole dish.

Carefully lower the casserole dish into your slow cooker. Now pour water around the casserole dish, to within 1' of the rim. Cover the slow cooker, set it to low, and let it cook for 3 to 3 1/2 hours.

YIELD: 6 servings, each with: 229 calories, 20g fat, 8g protein, 3g carbohydrate, trace dietary fibre, 3g usable carbs.

Southeast Asian Coconut Custard

I adapted this from a carby recipe in another slow cooker book. Maria, who tested it, says it's wonderful and also has a Latino feel to it. Look for shredded unsweetened coconut in Asian markets and health food stores.

5g sugar-free imitation honey
  (find this specialist ingredient online, try www.khwanabee.com)
1/2 tsp black treacle
1 1/2 tsps grated ginger root
1 tbsp (15ml) lime juice
425ml coconut milk
16g Splenda
1/4 tsp ground cardamom
1 tsp grated ginger root
120ml semi-skimmed milk
120ml double cream
1/2 tsp vanilla extract
4 eggs
35g shredded unsweetened coconut

Spray a 2 litre glass casserole dish with nonstick cooking spray. Put the honey and treacle in the casserole dish. Cover the casserole dish with clingfilm or a plate and microwave on high for 2 minutes. Add the 1 1/2 tsps ginger and lime juice and stir. Set aside.

In a mixing bowl, combine the coconut milk, Splenda, cardamom, the rest of the ginger, milk, cream, vanilla extract, and eggs. Whisk until well combined. Pour into the casserole dish. Cover the casserole dish with foil and secure it with a rubber band.

Put the casserole dish in your slow cooker and pour water around it, to within 3cm of the rim. Cover the slow cooker, set it to low, and let it cook for 3 to 4 hours.

Turn off the slow cooker, uncover, and let it cool till you can lift out the casserole dish without scalding your fingers. Chill overnight.

Before serving, stir the coconut in a dry frying pan over medium heat until it's golden. Remove the custard from the fridge and run a knife carefully around the edge. Put a plate on top and carefully invert the custard onto the plate. Sprinkle the toasted coconut on top.

YIELD: 8 servings, each with: 227 calories, 22g fat, 5g protein, 5g carbohydrate, 2g dietary fibre, 3g usable carbs.

☕ Maple Custard

This is for all you maple fans out there, and I know you're numbers are increasing!

355ml semi-skinned milk

120ml double cream

80ml sugar-free pancake syrup

8g Splenda

3 eggs

1 pinch salt

1 tsp vanilla extract

1/2 tsp maple extract

Simply whisk everything together and pour the mixture into a 2 litre glass casserole dish you've sprayed with oil to prevent sticking. Put the casserole dish in your slow cooker and pour water around it to within 3cm of the rim. Cover the slow cooker, set it to low, and let it cook for 4 hours.

When the time's up, turn off the slow cooker, remove the lid, and let it sit until the water is cool enough so that you can remove the casserole without risk of scalding. Chill well before serving.

YIELD: 6 servings, each with: 135 calories, 12g fat, 6g protein, 2g carbohydrate, 0g dietary fibre, 2g usable carbs. (Counts do not include polyols in pancake syrup.)

⛯ Maple-Pumpkin Custard

This is very much like the filling of a pumpkin pie, without the crust.
The pecans add a little textural contrast.

430g tinned pumpkin

235ml semi-skimmed milk

120ml double cream

80ml sugar-free pancake syrup

8g Splenda

1/2 tsp maple flavouring

3 eggs

1 pinch salt

1 tbsp (6g) mixed spice

35g chopped pecans

1 1/2 tsps butter

Whipped Topping (see recipe page 238)

In a mixing bowl, preferably one with a pouring lip, whisk together the pumpkin,
milk, cream, pancake syrup, Splenda, maple flavouring, eggs, salt, and pumpkin
pie spice.

Spray a 2 litre glass casserole dish with nonstick cooking spray. Pour the custard
mixture into it. Place it in your slow cooker. Now carefully fill the space around the
casserole with water, up to 3cm from the rim. Cover the slow cooker, set it to low,
and let it cook for 3 to 4 hours.

Remove the lid, turn off the slow cooker, and let it cool till you can remove the
casserole dish without scalding your fingers. Chill the custard for at least several hours.

Before serving, put the pecans and butter in a heavy frying pan over medium heat and
stir them for 5 minutes or so. Set aside. Also have the Whipped Topping made and
standing by.

Serve the custard with a dollop of Whipped Topping and 1 tbsp of toasted pecans on
each serving.

YIELD: 6 servings, each with: 341 calories, 31g fat, 7g protein, 10g carbohydrate,
3g dietary fibre, 7g usable carbs.

⌒ Apricot Custard

Don't go increasing the quantity of apricot preserves here. They're the biggest source of carbs. This dessert is yummy, though!

  100g low-sugar apricot preserves
  30ml lemon juice
  2 tsps Splenda
  355ml semi-skimmed milk
  120ml double cream
  4 eggs
  16g Splenda
  1/2 tsp almond extract
  1 pinch salt

Whisk together the preserves, lemon juice, and the 2 tsps of Splenda. Spread them over the bottom of a 2 litre glass casserole dish you've sprayed with oil to prevent sticking. Set aside.

Whisk together the milk, cream, eggs, 2/3 cup Splenda, almond extract, and salt. Pour into the prepared casserole gently, so as not to mix in the apricot preserves.

Place the casserole dish in your slow cooker. Pour water around the casserole to within 3cm of the rim. Cover the slow cooker, set it to low, and let it cook for 4 hours.

When the time's up, turn off the slow cooker, uncover it, and let it cool until you can remove the casserole dish without risk of scalding. Chill well before serving.

YIELD: 6 servings, each with: 165 calories, 12g fat, 7g protein, 7g carbohydrate, trace dietary fibre, 7g usable carbs.

⊙ Peaches with Butterscotch Sauce

These are delectable. You can serve them as is, with a little double cream, with Whipped Topping (see recipe page 238) – or, the Big Casino, with a scoop of low-carb vanilla ice cream.

> 450g frozen, unsweetened, sliced peaches
>
> 2 tsps lemon juice
>
> 8g Splenda
>
> 2 tbsps (40g) sugar-free imitation honey (this is a specialist ingredient, but you can buy it online, try www.khwanabee.com)
>
> 1/2 tsp black treacle
>
> 2 tbsps (30ml) double cream
>
> 1/4 tsp cinnamon
>
> 30g butter, melted
>
> Guar or xanthan

Place the peaches in your slow cooker. (I didn't even bother to thaw mine.)

In a bowl, stir together the lemon juice, Splenda, honey, treacle, cream, cinnamon, and butter. Pour the mixture over the peaches. Cover the slow cooker, set it to low, and let it cook for 6 hours.

Thicken the sauce to a creamy consistency with a little guar or xanthan and serve hot.

YIELD: 6 servings, each with: 86 calories, 6g fat, 1g protein, 9g carbohydrate, 2g dietary fibre, 7g usable carbs. (Analysis does not include polyols.)

Rhubarb Flummery

Because it's so sour, rhubarb is low-carb. This is a simple, old-fashioned dessert.

> 450g frozen rhubarb
> 12g Splenda
> 120ml water
> 1/8 tsp orange extract
> Guar or xanthan

Place the rhubarb in your slow cooker and stir in the Splenda, water, and orange extract. Cover the slow cooker, set it to low, and let it cook for 5 to 6 hours.

When the time's up, the rhubarb will be very soft. Mash it with a fork to a rough pulp. Thicken the sauce to a soft pudding consistency with guar or xanthan and serve hot or cold.

This dessert is great with a little double cream or Whipped Topping (see recipe page 238).

YIELD: 6 servings, each with: 16 calories, trace fat, trace protein, 4g carbohydrate, 1g dietary fibre, 3g usable carbs.

⛇ Hot Cinnamon Mocha

Assemble this in your slow cooker before going skating, caroling, or to a football game, and have a winter party waiting when you get home!

  1.75 litres chocolate-flavoured semi-skimmed milk

  2 cinnamon sticks

  3 tbsps (8g) instant coffee granules

  1 1/2 tsps vanilla extract

Combine everything in your slow cooker and give it a stir. Cover the slow cooker, set it to high, and let it cook for 3 hours. Turn the slow cooker to low and serve from the slow cooker.

If it's a grown-up party, put a bottle of Mockahlua on the side for spiking! (See recipe page 238.)

YIELD: 10 servings, each with: 92 calories, 4g fat, 10g protein, 5g carbohydrate, 2g dietary fibre, 3g usable carbs.

About Cheesecake

There were so many cheesecake recipes in *500 More Low-Carb Recipes* that I only did three for this book. However, cheesecake works very well in the slow cooker, so feel free to experiment with baking your favourite low-carb cheesecake recipes this way.

You'll notice I've called for light cream cheese and light sour cream in these recipes, instead of the full-fat versions. There's a reason for this: The light versions generally have no more carbohydrate than their full-fat counterparts, and they are, of course, lower calorie. I consider that a gain, and the cheesecakes come out very well. However, feel free to use the full-fat versions if you prefer.

Mochaccino Cheesecake

This cheesecake is extraordinary, as good as any dessert I ever had in a restaurant. This alone is a good enough reason to go buy a large, round slow cooker, and an 20cm cake tin to fit into it! It's also a good excuse to make some Mockahlua, but who needs an excuse to do that?

> Crisp Chocolate Crust (see recipe on the next page)
> 450g light cream cheese
> 1 egg
> 60ml double cream
> 40g + 2 tbsps (11g) unsweetened cocoa powder
> 12g Splenda
> 60ml Mockahlua (see recipe page 238)
> 2 tbsps (30ml) brewed coffee

Using your electric mixer, beat together the cream cheese, egg, and cream until quite smooth. (You'll need to scrape down the sides of the bowl several times.) Now beat in the cocoa powder, Splenda, Mockahlua, and coffee. When it's all well blended and very smooth, pour into the crust. Cover the cake tin tightly with foil, squeezing it in around the rim.

Take a big sheet of foil, at least 45 centimetres long, and roll it into a loose cylinder. Bend it into a circle and place it in the bottom of your slow cooker. (You're making a rack to put the pan on.) Pour 1cm of water in the bottom of the slow cooker, then put the pan on the donut of foil. Cover the slow cooker, set it to high, and let it cook for 3 to 4 hours.

Turn off the slow cooker, uncover, and let cool for at least 20 to 30 minutes before you try to remove the pan from the slow cooker. Chill well before serving.

It's nice to make the Whipped Topping (see recipe page 238), with a little Mockahlua in it, to serve on top of this, but it's hardly essential.

YIELD: 12 servings, each with: 284 calories, 24g fat, 11g protein, 10g carbohydrate, 4g dietary fibre, 6g usable carbs. (Analysis includes Crisp Chocolate Crust. You could cut this into eight, more generous servings if you'd like.)

Crisp Chocolate Crust

220g almonds
6g Splenda
2 squares bitter chocolate, melted
45g butter, melted
2 tbsps (16g) vanilla whey protein powder

Preheat the oven to 325°F.

Using the S-blade of your food processor, grind the almonds until they're the texture of corn meal. Add the Splenda and pulse to combine. Pour in the chocolate and butter and run processor till evenly distributed. (You may need to stop the processor and run the tip of a knife blade around the outer edge to get everything to combine properly.) Then add the protein powder and pulse again to combine.

Turn the mixture into an 20cm cake tin you've sprayed with oil to prevent sticking. Press firmly and evenly into place. Bake for 10 to 12 minutes in the preheated oven. Cool before filling.

YIELD: 12 servings, each with: 164 calories, 15g fat, 6g protein, 5g carbohydrate, 3g dietary fibre, 2g usable carbs.

New York–Style Cheesecake

You can top this with fruit if you like, but it's mighty good just as it is.

Biscuit Crust (see recipe on the next page)
450g light cream cheese
120g light sour cream
2 eggs
12g Splenda
2 tsps vanilla extract
1 pinch salt

Prepare the 'Graham' Crust and let it cool.

Using your electric mixer, beat the cheese, sour cream, and eggs until they're very smooth. (You'll need to scrape down the sides of the bowl at least a few times.) Now beat in the Splenda, vanilla extract, and salt. Pour into the waiting crust. Cover the pan tightly with foil, squeezing it in around the rim.

Take a big sheet of foil, at least 45 centimetres long, and roll it into a loose cylinder. Bend it into a circle, and place it in the bottom of your slow cooker. (You're making a rack to put the pan on.) Pour 1cm of water into your slow cooker, then put the pan on the donut of foil. Cover the slow cooker, set it to high, and let it cook for 3 to 4 hours.

Turn off the slow cooker, uncover, and let cool for at least 20 to 30 minutes before you try to remove the pan from the slow cooker. Chill well before serving.

YIELD: 12 servings, each with: 241 calories, 21g fat, 8g protein, 6g carbohydrate, 2g dietary fibre, 4g usable carbs. (You could cut this into eight, more generous servings if you'd like.)

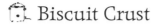 Biscuit Crust

180g almonds
2 tbsps (15g) wheat germ
2 tbsps (15g) wheat bran
3 tbsps (4.5g Splenda
1 pinch salt
80g butter, melted

Preheat the oven to 325°F.

Put the almonds in your food processor with the S-blade in place. Run it until they're ground to about the texture of corn meal. Add the wheat germ, wheat bran, Splenda, and salt and pulse to combine. Now turn on the processor and pour in the butter, running the processor until everything's well combined. (You may need to stop the processor and run a knife around the bottom edge to make sure all the dry ingredients come in contact with the butter.)

Turn this mixture out into an 20cm greased cake tin. Press firmly into place. Bake for 10 to 12 minutes, or until just turning gold around the edges. Cool before filling.

YIELD: 12 servings, each with: 144 calories, 14g fat, 3g protein, 4g carbohydrate, 2g dietary fibre, 2g usable carbs.

Peanut Butter Cheesecake

You can certainly eat this plain, but I like to top it with some sugar-free chocolate sauce. You can buy this online, or you could make some from the recipe on page 237. Or, for that matter, you could melt 175 to 225g of your favourite sugar-free chocolate bars and swirl them into the peanut butter batter before baking. The possibilities are endless!

Crisp Chocolate Crust (see recipe page 222) or Biscuit Crust
    (see recipe page 224)
450g light cream cheese
120g light sour cream
1 egg
200g natural peanut butter
    (salted is better than no-salt-added, here)
16g Splenda
1/2 tsps black treacle

Have your crust made and standing by.

Using your electric mixer, beat the cream cheese, sour cream, and egg until they're very smooth. (You'll want to scrape down the sides of the bowl several times.) Now beat in the peanut butter, Splenda, and treacle.

When the mixture is very smooth and well blended, pour it into the crust. Cover the pan tightly with foil, squeezing it in around the rim.

Take a big sheet of foil, at least 45cm long, and roll it into a loose cylinder. Bend it into a circle, and place it in the bottom of your slow cooker. (You're making a rack to put the pan on.) Pour 1cm of water into the slow cooker, then put the pan on the ring of foil. Cover the slow cooker, set it to high, and let it cook for 3 to 4 hours.

Turn off the slow cooker, uncover, and let cool for at least 20 to 30 minutes before you try to remove the pan from the slow cooker. Chill well before serving.

YIELD: 12 servings, each with: 364 calories, 32g fat, 13g protein, 10g carbohydrate, 4g dietary fibre, 6g usable carbs. (Analysis includes Crisp Chocolate Crust. Analysis does not include any chocolate sauce or melted chocolate you might add! You could cut this into eight, more generous servings if you'd like.)

CHAPTER TWELVE

Just A Few Extras...

This is where I've tucked the recipes that you need to make other recipes, but that aren't, themselves, slow cooker stuff. It just seemed easiest to put them all in one place, you know? Most of these have appeared in one or more of my previous cookbooks. And by the way, we didn't count these toward your grand total of 200 slow cooker recipes – that's why they're extras.

Dana's No-Sugar Ketchup

This recipe has appeared in all my cookbooks because ketchup is an essential ingredient in so many recipes, but store-bought ketchup usually has so much sugar. Recently, commercially-made low-carb ketchup has been appearing in the supermarkets. If you can get this, do so because food processors can get ingredients the home cook cannot, so store-bought low-carb ketchup is lower in carbs than this. If you can't find low-carb ketchup, however, this is easy to make, tastes great, and is about half the carbs of regular ketchup. Be aware that recipes that list ketchup as an ingredient are analyzed for this homemade version, so if you use commercial low-carb ketchup, the carb counts will be a tad lower.

100g tomato paste
150ml cider vinegar
75ml water
8g Splenda
20g finely chopped onion
2 cloves garlic
1 tsp salt
1/8 tsp ground allspice
1/8 tsp ground cloves
1/8 tsp pepper

Put everything in your blender and run it until the onion disappears. Scrape it into a container with a tight lid and store it in the refrigerator.

YIELD: Makes roughly 1 1/2 cups, or 12 servings of 2 tbsps, each with:
15 calories, trace fat, 1g protein, 5g carbohydrate, 1g fibre, 4g usable carbs.

Cocktail Sauce

You'll need this for the Easy Party Shrimp on page 24!

> 120g Dana's No-Sugar Ketchup (page 228)
>   or purchased low-carb ketchup
> 2 tsps prepared horseradish
> 1/4 tsp Tabasco sauce
> 1 tsp lemon juice

Combine all ingredients in a bowl and mix well.

YIELD: Makes about 1/2 cup. The whole batch contains: 142 calories, 1g fat, 5g protein, 36g carbohydrate, 6g dietary fibre, 30g usable carbs. Good thing you'll be sharing it! You can drop this carb count considerably by using commercially-made low-carb ketchup.

Florida Sunshine Tangerine Barbeque Sauce

The name of this sauce is partly from the tangerine note, which is unusual and delicious, but the name is also from the fact that this sauce is at least as hot as the Florida sun! It's especially good on poultry. You can use this in any of the recipes that call for barbeque sauce, or you can use the Kansas City–style sauce on the following page – this one's lower carb, but less traditional. Or, for that matter, you can use the newly available bottled low-carb barbeque sauce. You won't hurt my feelings.

> 350ml Diet Rite Tangerine Soda
> 6g Splenda
> 1 tbsp (7g) chilli powder
> 2 tsps black pepper
> 1 tsp ginger
> 1 tsp dry mustard
> 1 tsp onion salt
> 4 cloves garlic, crushed
> 1/2 tsp cayenne
> 1/2 tsp coriander
> 1/2 tsp red pepper flakes
> 1 bay leaf
> 120ml cider vinegar
> 1 tbsp (20g) sugar-free imitation honey
>   (find this specialist ingredient online, try www.khwanabee.com)
> 1 tbsp (15ml) Worcestershire sauce
> 180g Dana's No-Sugar Ketchup (page 228) or purchased
>   low-carb ketchup

Pour the soda into a nonreactive saucepan and turn the heat under it to medium-low. While that's heating, measure the other ingredients into the sauce. By the time you get to the ketchup, it should be simmering. Whisk everything together until smooth and let it simmer over lowest heat for a good 10 to 15 minutes.

YIELD: Makes about 3 cups, or 24 servings of 2 tbsps, each with: 11 calories, trace fat, trace protein, 3g carbohydrate, trace dietary fibre, 3g usable carbs.

Dana's 'Kansas City' Barbeque Sauce

If you like a smoky note in your barbeque sauce, add 1 tsp of liquid smoke flavouring to this. (Note: If you can get it locally, commercially-made low-carb barbeque sauce is likely to be lower carb than this recipe.)

30g butter
1 clove garlic
25g chopped onion
1 tbsp (15ml) lemon juice
240g Dana's No-Sugar Ketchup (page 228) or purchased
    low-carb ketchup
8g Splenda
1 tbsp (20g) black treacle
2 tbsps (30ml) Worcestershire sauce
1 tbsp (9g) chilli powder
1 tbsp (15ml) white vinegar
1 tsp pepper
1/4 tsp salt

Combine everything in a saucepan over low heat. Heat until the butter melts, stir the whole thing up, and let it simmer for 5 minutes or so. That's it!

YIELD: Roughly 1 3/4 cups, or 14 servings of 2 tbsps each, each with:
45 calories, 3g fat, 1g protein, 7g carbohydrate, 1g fibre, 6g usable carbs.

🝠 Piedmont Mustard Sauce

This bright-yellow sauce is heavy on the mustard, but completely free of tomato. Try it on Slow Cooker Pulled Pork (see recipe page 142).

> 125g yellow mustard
> 2 tbsps (30ml) lemon juice
> 2 tbsps (3g) Splenda
> 1 tbsp (15ml) white vinegar
> 1/4 tsp cayenne

Combine everything in a saucepan and simmer for 5 minutes over low heat.

YIELD: Makes roughly 3/4 cup, or 6 servings of 2 tbsps, each with: 17 calories, 1g fat, 1g protein, 2g carbohydrate, 1g dietary fibre, 1g usable carbs.

🝠 Eastern Carolina Vinegar Sauce

This is the traditional Eastern Carolina sauce for pulled pork. It's just sweetened vinegar with a good hint of hot pepper. It'll be great with your Slow Cooker Pulled Pork (see recipe page 142)!

> 120ml cider vinegar
> 1 1/2 tbsps (2g) Splenda
> 1/4 tsp black treacle
> 1 tsp red pepper flakes
> 1/4 tsp cayenne

Combine everything in a saucepan and simmer for 5 minutes over low heat.

YIELD: 6 servings, each with: 4 calories, trace fat, trace protein, 2g carbohydrate, trace dietary fibre, 2g usable carbs.

⊹ Hoisin Sauce

Hoisin sauce is sort of Chinese barbeque sauce, and it customarily contains a lot of sugar. It also doesn't usually have peanut butter in it, but it works quite well here. This is a repeat from *500 Low-Carb Recipes*, by the way.

> 4 tbsps (60ml) soy sauce
> 2 tbsps (35g) natural peanut butter
> 2 tbsps (3g) Splenda
> 2 tsps white vinegar
> 1 clove garlic
> 2 tsps dark sesame oil
> 1/8 tsp five-spice powder

Just assemble everything in your blender and blend till it's smooth. Store it in a tightly lidded jar in the fridge. Feel free to double or triple this, if you like.

YIELD: Makes roughly 1/3 cup, or 6 servings of about 1 tbsp, each with: 52 calories, 4g fat , 2g protein, 2g carbohydrate, trace dietary fibre, 1g usable carbs.

⊹ Low-Carb Teriyaki Sauce

There's now commercial low-carb teriyaki sauce on the market, but I like this better, and it's so easy to make, why wouldn't I? Why wouldn't you?

> 120ml soy sauce
> 60ml dry sherry
> 1 clove garlic, crushed
> 2 tbsps (3g) Splenda
> 1 tbsp (8g) grated ginger root

Combine all the ingredients. Refrigerate until ready to use.

YIELD: Makes 3/4 cup, or 12 servings of 1 tbsp, each with: 13 calories, trace fat, 1g protein, 1g carbohydrate, trace dietary fibre, 1g usable carbs.

Classic Rub

This barbeque rub first appeared in *The Low-Carb Barbeque Book*, and it's a great choice in any recipe that calls for barbeque seasoning.

6g Splenda
1 tbsp (18g) seasoned salt
1 tbsp (8g) garlic powder
1 tbsp (18g) celery salt
1 tbsp (9g) onion powder
2 tbsps (14g) paprika
1 tbsp (9g) chilli powder
2 tsps pepper
1 tsp lemon pepper
1 tsp ground sage
1 tsp mustard
1/2 tsp thyme
1/2 tsp cayenne

Simply stir everything together and store in an airtight container.

YIELD: Makes 13 tbsps of rub, each with: 13 calories, trace fat, 1g protein, 2g carbohydrate, 1g dietary fibre, 1g usable carbs.

 Cajun Seasoning

This New Orleans–style seasoning, originally from *500 Low-Carb Recipes*, is good sprinkled over chicken, steak, pork, fish – just about anything. It will also work in any recipe in this book that calls for Cajun seasoning. But if you'd rather use purchased seasoning, go for it.

> 2 1/2 tbsps (18g) paprika
> 2 tbsps (30g) salt
> 2 tbsps (16g) garlic powder
> 1 tbsp (6g) pepper
> 1 tbsp (9g) onion powder
> 1 tbsp (5g) cayenne
> 1 tbsp (4g) dried oregano
> 1 tbsp (3g) dried thyme

Combine all ingredients thoroughly and store in an airtight container.

YIELD: Makes 2/3 cup. The whole batch contains: 187 calories, 4g fat, 8g protein, 37g carbohydrate, 9g dietary fibre, 28g usable carbs. (Considering how spicy this is, you're unlikely to use more than a tsp or two at a time. One tsp has 1 gram of carbohydrate, with a trace of fibre.)

Adobo Seasoning

Adobo is a popular seasoning in Latin America and the Caribbean. It's available at many supermarkets, in the spice aisle or the international aisle. But if you can't find it, it's really easy to make.

    10 tsps garlic powder
    5 tsps dried oregano
    5 tsps pepper
    2 1/2 tsps paprika
    5 tsps salt

Simply measure everything into a bowl, stir, and store in a lidded shaker jar.

YIELD: Makes a little over 1/2 cup, or about 48 servings of 1/2 tsp, each with: 3 calories, trace fat, trace protein, 1g carbohydrate, trace dietary fibre, 1g usable carbs.

Garam Masala

This is an Indian spice blend used in several of the curries in this book. You may well be able to buy perfectly lovely garam masala already made at a local Asian market or big supermarket – I can! But if you can't, you can easily make your own.

    2 tbsps (6g) ground cumin
    2 tbsps (10g) ground coriander
    2 tbsps (6g) ground cardamom
    1 1/2 tbsps black pepper
    4 tsps ground cinnamon
    1/2 tsp ground cloves
    1 tsp ground nutmeg

Simply combine everything and store in an airtight container.

YIELD: Makes roughly 9 tbsps, each with: 19 calories, 1g fat, 1g protein, 4g carbohydrate, 1g dietary fibre, 3g usable carbs.

⊡ Sugar–Free Chocolate Sauce

This is as good as any sugar-based chocolate sauce you've ever had, if I do say so myself. Which I do. Don't try to make this with Splenda; it won't work. The polyol sweetener somehow makes the water and the chocolate combine. It's chemistry, or magic, or some wierd thing. You will very probably need to order maltitol. Just do a web search under 'low carbohydrate,' and you'll find dozens of webites ready to ship anything your heart desires.

> 75ml water
> 4 tbsps unsweetened baking chocolate
> 100g maltitol
> 45g butter
> 1/4 tsp vanilla

Put the water and chocolate in a glass measuring cup and microwave on high for 1 to 1 1/2 minutes, or until the chocolate has melted. Stir in the maltitol and microwave on high for another 3 minutes, stirring halfway through. Stir in the butter and vanilla.

NOTE: This works beautifully with maltitol. However, when I tried to make it with other granular polyols – erythritol, isomalt – it started out fine but crystallized and turned grainy as it cooled. I'd stick with maltitol.

YIELD: Makes roughly 1 cup, or 8 servings of 2 tbsps, each with: 75 calories, 8g fat, 1g protein, 2g carbohydrate, 1g dietary fibre, 1g usable carbs. (This does not include the maltitol.)

Mockahlua

This recipe originally appeared in *500 Low-Carb Recipes*, but because I've included it in some recipes in the dessert chapter I thought I'd better repeat it! This recipe makes quite a lot, but don't worry about that; 100-proof vodka's a very good preservative. Your Mockahlua will keep indefinitely.

> 350ml water
> 75g Splenda
> 3 tbsps (8g) instant coffee granules
> 1 tsp vanilla extract
> 1 bottle (750ml) strong vodka (Use the cheap stuff.)

In a large pitcher or measuring cup, combine the water, Splenda, coffee granules, and vanilla extract. Stir until the coffee and Splenda are completely dissolved.

Pour the mixture through a funnel into a 1.5 or 2 litre bottle. (A clean 1.5 litre wine bottle works fine, so long as you've saved the cork.) Pour in the vodka. Cork and shake well.

YIELD: 32 servings of 1 1/2 ounces – a standard 'shot,' each with: 53 calories, 0g fat, trace protein, trace carbohydrate, 0g dietary fibre, trace usable carbs.

Whipped Topping

I keep repeating this recipe, but then, it's a wonderful, classic whipped cream topping for any dessert.

> 235ml double cream, chilled
> 3 tsps sugar-free vanilla instant pudding mix

Simply whip the cream with the pudding mix. Use your electric mixer, or, if you like, a whisk – neither a blender nor a food processor will work. Stop whipping as soon as your topping is nice and thick, or you'll end up with vanilla butter!

If you make this ahead of time, refrigerate it until you're ready to serve dessert.

YIELD: 8 servings, each with: 104 calories, 11g fat, 1g protein, 1g carbohydrate, 0g dietary fibre, 1g usable carbs.

⊓ Cauli-Rice

With thanks to Fran McCullough! I got this idea from her book *Living Low-Carb*, and it's served me very well indeed.

1/2 head cauliflower

Simply put the cauliflower through your food processor using the shredding blade. This gives a texture that is remarkably similar to rice. You can steam this, microwave it, or even sauté it in butter. Whatever you do, though, don't overcook it! I usually put mine in a microwaveable casserole with a lid, add a couple of tbsps of water, and microwave it for 7 minutes on high.

YIELD: This makes about 3 cups, or at least 3 to 4 servings. Assuming 3 servings, each with: 24 calories, trace fat, 2g protein, 5g carbohydrate, 2g dietary fibre, 3g usable carbs.

⊓ Fauxtatoes

This is a wonderful substitute for mashed potatoes if you want something to put a fabulous sour cream gravy on! Feel free, by the way, to use frozen cauliflower instead. It works quite well here.

1 head cauliflower or 700g frozen cauliflower
60g butter

Steam or microwave the cauliflower until it's soft. Drain it thoroughly and put it through the blender or food processor until it's well pureed. Add the butter and salt and pepper to taste.

YIELD: 6 servings, each with: 72 calories, 8g fat, trace protein, 1g carbohydrate, trace dietary fibre, trace usable carbs. (This makes six generous servings.)

 The Ultimate Fauxtatoes

I'm not crazy about Ketatoes by themselves, but added to pureed cauliflower Fauxtatoes, they add a potato-y flavour and texture that is remarkably convincing! This is a killer side dish with many of your slow cooker main dishes.

> 1/2 head cauliflower
> 50g Ketatoes mix
> 120ml boiling water
> 30g butter

Trim the bottom of the stem of your cauliflower and whack the rest of the head into chunks. Put them in a microwaveable casserole dish with a lid. Add a couple of tbsps of water, cover, and microwave on high for 8 to 9 minutes.

While that's happening, measure your Ketatoes mix and boiling water into a mixing bowl and whisk together.

When the microwave beeps, pull out your cauliflower – it should be tender. Drain it well and put it in either your food processor, with the S-blade in place, or in your blender. Either way, puree the cauliflower until it's smooth. Transfer the pureed cauliflower to the mixing bowl and stir the cauliflower and Ketatoes together well. Add the butter and stir till it melts. Add salt and pepper to taste and serve.

YIELD: 4 servings, each with: 140 calories, 5g fat, 10g protein, 14g carbohydrate, 8g dietary fibre, 6g usable carbs.

Index

Acknowledgments

A few quick thank you's here:

To my darling friend Maria Vander Vloedt, who tested many, many recipes for this book. She's the perfect tester: She's smart and funny and reliable, she knows how to cook, she can follow instructions but make constructive suggestions when they're needed, she eats low-carb, and she has a husband and five kids to try my recipes out on! Thanks, Maria.

Also to my sister Kim, who is always up for a new recipe, and my pal Ray Stevens, who tested a bunch when crunch time rolled around: Thanks, guys!

As always, to my husband, Eric Schmitz. Thank God I married him, I could never find another person with his combination of skills in the open job market. All this, and he's nice to have around the house, too.

And to my editor, Holly, for browbeating me into writing this book. It's been a lot cooler than I expected.

500 Low-Carb Recipes

ISBN 1-84092-431-4
£8.99
Paperback, 500 pages
Available wherever books are sold

Okay, you've finally done it. You've gone low-carb! And no matter which one of the many low-carbohydrate diets you've chosen, you've discovered the joys of weight loss without hunger, not to mention energy that never seems to quit, and rapidly improving health.

Just one little problem: If you have to face one more day of eggs for breakfast, tuna salad for lunch, and a burger without the bun for dinner, you're going to scream. Worse, you're going to order a pizza!

Rejoice, my low-carb friend. Help is here; you hold it in your hands. In this book you'll find options galore. You'll find dozens upon dozens of new things to do with your protein foods and vegetables and you'll find recipes for foods you thought you'd never, ever be able to eat on your low-carb diet:

• Cinnamon Raisin Bread • Feta-Spinach Salmon Roast
• Sour Cream Coffee Cake • Obscenely Rich Shrimp
• Chocolate Mousse to DIE For • Mum's Chocolate Chip Cookies • Mockahlua Cheesecake
• French Toast • Heroin Wings • Sugar-Free Ketchup and Barbeque Sauce

You'll also learn more about how to count carbs and read labels, as well as get an overview of low-carb ingredients. You'll get the lowdown on all those new low-carb speciality products flooding the market. And, of course, you get 14 chapters of recipes, covering everything from Hors d'oeuvres, Snacks and Party Nibbles, to Breads, Muffins, Cereals and Other Grainy Things.

You'll find cookies, cakes and other sweets. Plus more recipes for main dishes and side dishes than you'll ever be able to eat your way through – everything from down-home cooking to ethnic fare; from quick-and-easy week-night meals to knock-their-socks-off party food. So say goodbye to boredom, and hello to exciting low-carb meals every day! Whether you're a kitchen novice or a gourmet chef, you'll find dozens of recipes to suit your tastes, budget and lifestyle.

15-Minute Low-Carb Recipes

ISBN: 1-84092-436-5
£9.99
Paperback; 256 pages

Available wherever books are sold

Yikes! It's 6:30 p.m and you've just walked through the door after a long day at work, plus a couple of errands. You're tired, you're hungry – and before you can get your coat off, the family has started asking, 'What's for dinner?'

In the past, you would have started boiling water for some quick pasta-and-cheese, or warmed up a frozen pizza. Hungry and busy though you may be, you really don't want to trade your weight loss, high energy and improved health for a quick-and-carb-y supper. What, oh what, to do?

Relax! No, really, sit down, relax, take a deep breath, and flip through *15-Minute Low-Carb Recipes*. You'll find dozens of wonderful family dishes that take no more than fifteen minutes to make, prep time included. You'll even find stuff you'd be happy to serve to company, should you be so brave as to invite people over on a week-night!

So grab this book, and simplify your life. Instead of another round of plain steak or bunless fast food burgers, you could be eating:

**Rosemary-Ginger Ribs with Apricot Glaze * Cranberry Burgers * Eggs Fu Yong
* Cumin Mushrooms * Swordfish Vera Cruz * Chicken Chilli Verde
* Aladdin Salad * Beef and Bacon 'Rice' with Pine Nuts
* Mexican Cabbage Soup * Aegean Chicken * Mushroom 'Risotto'**

And much, much more – all with the carbohydrate, fibre and usable carb counts already calculated for you. What could be easier?

The Low-Carb Barbecue Book

ISBN: 1-84092-480-2
£7.99
Paperback; 256 pages

Available wherever books are sold

BARBECUE!

Admit it, your mouth is watering at the very word. Who doesn't love a slab of succulent, smoky ribs, or moist, juicy chicken, hot off the grill and slathered in a sweet-and-tangy sauce?

Barbecue, with its generous helpings of protein, seems ideal for us low-carb types. But just take one glance at the ingredients of your favourite barbecue sauces and rubs – you might as well be pouring pancake syrup on your dinner! Then there are those traditional barbecue sides – potato salad, chips, sugary coleslaw, onion rings and gallons of beer. Can't you feel your jeans getting tighter just thinking about it?

Well, help is at hand! In this book you'll find recipes for barbecue sauces that will turn your pork, chicken or beef into pure ambrosia, and every single one of them contains half the carbs of traditional barbecue sauce, or less! You'll find sugarless rubs and seasonings of every description, and mopping sauces to keep your meat moist and tender during that long, slow smoking.

Don't have time for traditional smoked barbecue? You'll find new, delicious, low-carb options for grilled meats, poultry and fish, too. Plus, low-carb onion rings, hush puppies, salads, slaws, grilled veggies – everything you need to turn your barbecue into a low-carb summer feast. Even low-carb versions of your favourite summer cocktails!

Recipes include:

Kansas City Barbeque Sauce * North Carolina Pulled Pork * Maple-Balsamic Glazed Salmon * Five-Spice Beef Ribs * Chipotle-Garlic Grilled Asparagus Bourbon-Treacle Barbeque Sauce * Apple-Maple Brined Ribs Thai Grilled Chicken * Bodacious Brined and Barbequed Beef Brisket

So fire up the grill! It's time to barbecue!

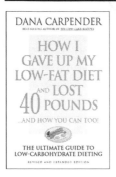

How I Gave Up My Low-Fat Diet and Lost 40 Pounds

ISBN 1-59233-040-1
$14.95/£9.99/$23.95 CAN
Paperback, 312 pages
Available wherever books are sold

It's time to go low-carb! Low-carbohydrate diets burn off twice the fat of low-fat or low-calorie diets, and they do it without making you starve. Here's the lowdown on how and why low-carbohydrate dieting works, not just for weight loss, but for dramatic health improvement. Without using boring, confusing medical jargon, I'll show you surprising research proving that carbohydrates, not fat, are the biggest culprit in causing diseases like diabetes, cancer, and coronary artery disease. Then I'll explain to you not one, but more than a half-a-dozen different approaches to cutting the carbs, and give you the information you need to mix-and-match these plans to come up with a low-carbohydrate diet you can live with for the rest of your long and healthy life.

So come on! Let me show you how to:

- Lose weight without hunger!
- Have the energy of a kid again!
- Eat more wonderful, real food than you ever thought possible!

All the while improving your cholesterol and triglycerides, lowering your blood pressure, and cutting your risk of diabetes and cancer. Let me tell you *How I Gave Up My Low-Fat Diet and Lost 40 Pounds . . . and How You Can Too!*

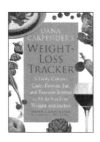

Dana Carpender's Weight-Loss Tracker

ISBN: 1-59233-151-3
$6.95/$9.95 CAN
Paperback; 128 pages
Available wherever books are sold

Struggling with your weight? Write down what you eat and watch the pounds disappear!

Most people think that meeting their weight loss goal begins and ends with what they put in their mouths. In reality, the majority of people who lose weight and keep it off have something else in common – they keep careful track of what they eat, especially carbs. *Dana Carpender's Weight-Loss Tracker* gives you all the information and space you need to write it all down: what you eat, how much, and each food's nutrient counts, including fibre, fat, protein, calories, and carbs. You can also record how much exercise you do and whether you're reaching your general health goals. Keeping track of this information will help you start your weight loss journey or bust out of a plateau!